PATHWAYS TO SPIRITUALITY AND HEALING

PATHWAYS TO
Spirituality
and Healing

Embracing Life
and Each Other
in the Face of a
Serious Illness

Alexa W. Umbreit, RNC, MS, CHTP, and
Mark S. Umbreit, PhD

*Fairview Press, in cooperation with
the Center for Spirituality and Healing,
University of Minnesota, Minneapolis*

Established in 1995 within the University of Minnesota's Academic Health Center, the Center for Spirituality and Healing's mission is to promote interdisciplinary education, research, and patient care that integrate biomedical, complementary, cross-cultural, and spiritual aspects of care.

Library of Congress Cataloging-in-Publication Data
Umbreit, Alexa W.
  Pathways to spirituality and healing : embracing life and each other in the face of a serious illness / Alexa W. Umbreit and Mark S. Umbreit.
    p. cm.
Includes bibliographical references.
  ISBN 1-57749-110-6 (alk. paper)
1. Sick--Religious life. 2. Spiritual healing. I. Umbreit, Mark S., 1949- II. Title.
  BL625.9.S53 .U53 2002
  291.4'42--dc21   2002001212

ISBN-13: 978-1-57749-110-1
First Printing: March 2002
Printed in the United States of America
Cover design by Laurie Ingram

The four essential steps of centering prayer, on page 61, were developed by Father Thomas Keating and presented in a pamphlet entitled *The Method of Centering Prayer,* published by Contemplative Outreach, Ltd., P.O. Box 737, Butler, N.J. 07405. Reprinted with permission.

Disclaimer
This publication is designed to provide accurate and authoritative information in regard to the subject matter covered. It is sold with the understanding that the publisher is not engaged in the provision or practice of medical, nursing, or professional healthcare advice or services in any jurisdiction. If medical advice or other professional assistance is required, the services of a qualified and competent professional should be sought. Fairview Press is not responsible or liable, directly or indirectly, for any form of damages whatsoever resulting from the use (or misuse) of information contained in or implied by these documents.

For a free current catalog of Fairview Press titles, please call toll-free 1-800-544-8207. Or visit our Web site at www.fairviewpress.org.

We dedicate this book to Jenni and Laura, our daughters.
May the compassion in their hearts and the Creator-given wisdom
in their souls continue to guide them in the journey of life.

Go forth in peace.
Be still within yourself, and know that the trail is beautiful.
May the winds be gentle upon your face,
and your direction be straight and true as the flight of the eagle.
Walk in beauty and harmony with God and all people.

– a Navajo blessing

CONTENTS

FOREWORD

Pathways to Spirituality and Healing is a generous and tender offering. It reveals the intimate anguish that arises when we are pressed tightly and unexpectedly against the membrane of impermanence, illness, and death. More specifically, it opens doorways and throws open the windows of our souls to allow the fresh, clean winds of curiosity, love, devotion, and healing to blow through us and grant us peace. The wisdom in these words is clearly spoken and hard won; it grew in the soil of two hearts beating together, a symphony of hope in the midst of the seduction of despair. This book is an act of love. Alexa and Mark have blessed us all with an astonishing gift. Use it well, and you will be changed.

WAYNE MULLER
pastor and best-selling author of
How, Then, Shall We Live?,
Legacy of the Heart, and *Sabbath*

ACKNOWLEDGMENTS

This book is grounded in our personal journey toward healing and strength, toward a deeper and more inclusive experience of spirituality. Yet, our journey is intertwined with lives of many others in similar circumstances, all of whom have touched our lives deeply.

We want to first acknowledge the tremendous support, compassion, and kindness offered by our immediate and extended family, friends in our support groups, neighbors, friends in our church, and colleagues at work.

After we published two booklets on spirituality and healing, Mary Jo Kreitzer, director of the Center for Spirituality and Healing at the University of Minnesota, and Lane Stiles, director of Fairview Press, encouraged us to expand them into this book. We thank Mary Jo and Lane for their encouragement and support. We would also like to thank Stephanie Billecke at Fairview Press for her editing and final preparation of the manuscript.

The feedback we received from numerous individuals who reviewed the manuscript—including therapists, survivors, and friends—was tremendously helpful. A special thanks to Anne Alwell, Marilyn Armour, Julie Andrus, Heather Burns, Bill Bradshaw, Bob Coates, Liz Jamieson, and Betty Vos. We also want to thank the many survivors and their significant others who encouraged us to pursue this book.

Finally, we want to acknowledge the profound impact that so many gifted teachers and authors have had on our lives.

The beauty and guidance we have found in our own religion and in many other spiritual traditions have deeply enriched our lives and provided pathways to embrace and experience the precious gift of each moment, the joy of relationships, the beauty of creation, and the hope for greater compassion, peace, and justice among all peoples of the world.

Finding hope in the face of serious illness is no simple task. As the normal patterns of our lives become shattered, we feel increasingly vulnerable and powerless. Anger can consume us. Our sense of time and the busyness of our lives can change dramatically. People and relationships we have often taken for granted may now become far more important. Issues related to life's deeper meaning and our purpose on this planet can begin to consume far more of our energy. We often crave a return to so-called normal life, struggling with the powerful drive to live in denial of how fundamentally our lives have changed in the wake of serious illness or loss.

For many of us, the burden becomes more than we can bear. Feeling little power to affect what is now happening in our lives, we often become depressed and incapacitated, unable to conduct even the most mundane tasks. When an illness becomes increasingly severe, our close personal relationships can fall apart.

Few people realize that a patient's spouse or partner can suffer as much as the patient. While denial will often initially kick in for the person diagnosed with a life-threatening illness, the spouse or partner feels overwhelmed and terrified. Moreover, he or she is confronted with numerous immediate tasks and practical considerations. With such heightened stress in the relationship, some couples grow closer and treasure each moment, while others grow apart and even separate.

This book comes out of our own life's journey, grounded in my diagnosis of breast cancer and the confrontation with death. The story of that life-altering experience provides a specific context for our discussion of spirituality and healing. The characteristics of our journey overlap heavily with, yet are also distinct from, the journeys of those struggling with AIDS, cancer, ALS (Lou Gehrig's disease), fibromyalgia, multiple sclerosis, and many other serious illnesses. Most of what we present in this book should be of practical value to anyone in the midst of severe stress or experiencing grief over the loss of a loved one. In all of these circumstances we each hunger for healing and strength.

By sharing our personal story, we wish to offer hope and practical tools that may empower others facing a serious illness, both patients and support persons. This book provides a road map for making this journey without denying or minimizing its pain. The book is not prescriptive; rather, it invites you to search out, try, and experience options that best fit with your personal needs, cultural context, and spiritual or religious traditions.

We encourage you to lean gently into your emotional and physical pain, become intimately acquainted with it, even befriend the pain and learn to work with it. Try to avoid giving it more power because of the heightened fear and anxiety that you are likely experiencing.

It is our hope that this book can help you take the initial steps toward healing and spirituality. Once you find a path that feels right to you, in-depth study and practice will be required. For that reason, in the telling of our story, we share with you numerous books, meditations, and other resources that may deepen your experience.

Each personal journey is unique. Many stories of serious illness would be far worse than our own, while other journeys would not be as devastating. For all, the experience of fear, uncertainty, vulnerability, and powerlessness is the common thread.

> *When we directly face what frightens us,*
> *we often discover our own capacity to survive*
> *whatever we have been given. The more we are*
> *present with ourselves in fear, without withdrawing,*
> *hiding out, or armoring ourselves, the more trust*
> *we develop in our own resources, our own*
> *creativity, resilience, and wisdom.*
>
> – *Wayne Muller,* Legacy of the Heart

Many books for people encountering serious illness do not address the full emotional and physical pain frequently experienced. We have intentionally included the full impact of our own experience in the belief that people have far more strength and resilience than most well-intentioned healthcare providers and other caregivers often assume.

We found far more strength and hope within ourselves than we thought we were capable of, given such a devastating diagnosis. We have come to firmly believe that the first step on the pathway to spirituality and healing is to accept and learn to work with, rather than deny and fight against, the very terror that one faces. Through doing so, the pathway to embracing the precious and fragile gift of life, to experiencing joy and fulfillment in the midst of trauma and uncertainty, becomes far more accessible.

*Through the gateway of feeling your weakness
  lies your strength.
Through the gateway of feeling your pain
  lies your pleasure and joy.
Through the gateway of feeling your fear
  lies your security and safety.
Through the gateway of feeling your loneliness
  lies your capacity to have fulfillment, love
  and companionship.
Through the gateway of feeling your hopelessness
  lies true and justified hope.
Through the gateway of accepting the lacks in your
  childhood lies your fulfillment now.*

— *Eva Pierrakos*

Our story is told across three chapters.

Chapter 1, "Confronting Death and Loss," shares the devastating story of my diagnosis and treatment, as well as their impact on our relationship and our family.

Chapter 2, "Pathways to Healing," identifies helpful information we discovered at various points along our journey, both as individuals and as a couple. We not only suggest guidelines for how to be more actively involved in your own healing process, but also describe methods and paths that can enhance self-healing and well being. These include massage; guided imagery; Healing Touch; prayer and meditation; traditional Eastern healing movement techniques such as yoga, qigong, and tai chi; nutrition; and music.

Chapter 3, "Pathways to Spirituality," shares jewels of wisdom from diverse faith traditions, including Christianity,

Judaism, Islam, Native American spirituality, Buddhism, Hinduism, and Taoism. While we remain firmly anchored in our own Christian heritage, we have been profoundly influenced during our darkest moments by the wisdom and practices of many spiritual traditions.

At the end of this book is a glossary of terms related to spirituality and healing, as well as a list of books, videotapes, and audiotapes related to physical, emotional, and spiritual healing and growth. We found these to be extremely helpful during our journey. In the early stages of my diagnosis and treatment no such list was available, so we did an enormous amount of research and reading to identify a rich assortment of resources.

In our journey we seek balance, not perfection—balance in the physical, emotional, spiritual, and relational dimensions of our lives. Our first and continuing steps along the pathway to spirituality and healing have been anchored in the well-known serenity prayer, which has brought strength to so many throughout the world over the years. We offer an altered version of this prayer as the foundation on which everything in this book is grounded:

> God grant me the serenity to accept that which I cannot control in myself, in others, or in the circumstances that I am faced with.

> Grant me the courage to change that which I can, and to take responsibility for my feelings and actions as I face the people and circumstances in my life at this moment.

Grant me the wisdom to know the difference.

Our story is simply our story. We are neither experts nor saints. We are survivors. We hope that sharing our lives with you in this way will encourage you to seek your own pathways to healing and spirituality. We also urge you to share your own stories of struggle, transformation, and joy.

We wish you strength and peace in your own journey toward a deeper understanding of spirituality and healing. May your heart be open to fully embracing the precious and fragile gift of life; the joy of family, friends, and each other; the incredible beauty and mystery of the universe; and the creator-given gifts of healing to be found within every one of us.

CHAPTER ONE

Confronting
Death and Loss

Diagnosis

I had been waiting over twenty years. But now that Jenni was nineteen, Laura was sixteen, and Mark's graduate education was well behind him, I finally had the chance to work toward a personal goal: a master's degree in nursing. The year 1994 looked promising. At age forty-three, I had put in my application to graduate school. Though nervous about taking classes again after all these years—along with working—I was charging ahead with grad-level statistics, a difficult but required course that I wanted to get out of the way as soon as possible.

It was during that first week of class when I noticed it: unusual sensations on one side of my right breast. The area was neither inflamed nor visibly swollen, but it was tender and felt full. I pulled out my medical texts to see if these symptoms might have any connection to breast cancer. The books reminded me of what, as a nurse, I already knew: breast cancer is rarely painful. Since I was due for a mammogram anyway, I made an appointment with a radiologist and another with my family physician.

I wasn't worried, but I had reason to be sensitive about the issue. My father's sister and my childhood friend had both developed breast cancer. But my symptoms were nothing like theirs, and—no surprise—my mammograms showed nothing unusual, not even the "targeted" ones. Current and previous X-rays looked the same. There was no palpable mass.

My family physician was not sure what was going on. He suggested I consult with a surgeon. So I did.

The surgeon didn't know what was going on either.

What now? Two choices were given to me. I could "watch it" for a month or two and see what happened—maybe it would resolve on its own, or maybe I was going into menopause. Or the surgeon could arrange a biopsy of the area and see if anything showed up. It was up to me.

I wasn't all that concerned, because my symptoms were uncommon and mild. True, I wasn't keen about having a needle stuck into my breast, but something inside me—perhaps the illnesses of my aunt and my childhood friend—said *just have the biopsy and be done with it.*

A few weeks later, I was back at the radiologist's. First, a couple of ultrasounds and another mammogram. Then the doctor anesthetized the biopsy site—which didn't feel very good—and assured me that I wouldn't feel any more pain. A large bore needle punctured my breast. Burning pain filled my chest and brought tears to my eyes.

"That hurts!" I couldn't hold back.

"Well, it shouldn't!" He withdrew the needle and I caught my breath.

"Doctor," I asked, "have you ever had this done?" Of course he had not.

Five times he inserted the needle to obtain the required tissue. The pain was shocking. My breast was now bruised and even more tender. I was exhausted when Mark brought me home. His presence during this diagnostic test, even as he sat in the waiting room, was so helpful. My surgeon would call with the results in twenty-four hours.

When we arrived at our house, Mark needed to finish packing for an important business trip he had planned for the next day. Mark now wondered if he should cancel the trip. He said he wanted to be with me when I got the results. I thanked him for his concern, but was confident that whatever it was, it wasn't cancer. That's what my physicians thought, too. My symptoms were atypical, I had no risk factors, no genetic predisposition, and I was too young.

Besides, I knew the trip was important to him.

"I'll be fine, Mark. In fact, I am fine—just sore. You go. It'll be fine."

So Mark left for Albuquerque the next morning and I went in to work. Instead of waiting at home for the call, I figured that doing what I loved best—being a nurse—would keep me occupied and make the time fly.

But twenty-four hours passed without a call from the surgeon. I called the office in the morning: "The doctor is in surgery and we don't know when she'll be out." I called again from work, mid-afternoon: "The doctor is still in surgery and we don't know when she'll be out." I asked for the results of my biopsy: "I'm sorry. We can't give them to you"—I knew that, but I just wanted to get this thing over with—"but the surgeon will want to talk with you." I knew that phrase. It was a kind of code.

I panicked. The receiver rattled its way into the cradle. My heart was racing and a sick feeling washed over me. Was the impossible coming true? What would I do if this were really breast cancer? I ran to the restroom and cried.

I dragged myself through to the end of the shift, then quickly retreated to my home and waited. Still no call from the surgeon. Just before closing, I called the office again: "The doctor is in surgery and we don't know when she'll be out."

A couple of hours later, I rang the answering service: "We only page the physician in a true emergency."

Finally, I got angry. "This *is* an emergency and I need to talk to the doctor as soon as possible!"

Meanwhile, my daughter Jenni came over with her boyfriend. We waited together, full of fear yet trying hard to look calm.

It was 8:00 P.M. before the surgeon finally called back. She asked me to come into her office the next day to talk about the results.

"I can't wait that long," I said. "It's been over twenty-four hours, I've been trying to reach you all day, and I need to know now." I could deal with facts a lot better than my imagination. Not knowing was worse than any bad news.

The surgeon paused. "Are you alone, Alexa, or is there someone with you?"

"My daughter's sitting right next to me at the kitchen table."

"The biopsy shows cancer, Alexa. I am very sorry."

I heard the words as if through a dream. Suddenly everything stopped—my breath, my eyes, my jaw, my hand on the telephone all froze in position. I heard the news, yet didn't hear it. It echoed in my mind but would not register. There was no place to store such information—a square peg among round holes.

Yet, somehow, I managed to exhale. To blink. Clear my throat. And, over the next forty-five minutes, to ask questions of my doctor and discuss treatment options. Dr. J. was compassionate and attentive. She said she would call me in a day or so, after I had time to take all this in, and together we would plan the surgery.

I thanked her and hung up the phone.

Jenni had been sobbing. I reached out to my daughter and held her close. For a long time we cried on each other's shoulders.

Again the phone rang. I picked it up. "Hello?"

It was Mark calling from his hotel in Albuquerque to ask about the test results.

"Are you sitting down?" Now it was my turn to pass on the news. "I have cancer," I said.

The phone crackled in silence for a moment, then Mark spoke. "Oh, God. I'm so sorry."

"I need to have surgery," I said, wondering how I could breathe and think and talk about it at all. "And if the cancer has spread, I may even need to see an oncologist after that. We'll have to figure out a course of treatment."

There. The news was out. It was what I had feared most, but at least now I knew.

The terror that Mark felt upon hearing those words must have been indescribable. Not disbelief, not even anger initially. Just raw, naked fear, vulnerability, hopelessness! We talked and cried together. Mark told me that he would immediately reschedule a flight back home, inevitably a "red eye" special traveling in the early hours of the next day. Only Mark can fully convey the enormous impact of the news:

As the phone call eventually ended and I hung up the receiver, a wave of anger pulsated through my body with such intensity that I felt even more frightened. I cursed, I pounded the pillows on the bed, I cried from the depths of my soul—not a gentle sobbing, but a gut-wrenching expression of the terror I felt within every fiber of my being. The anger that erupted so quickly and the pain that I experienced so intensely began to subside after twenty minutes or so.

I had to mobilize every ounce of my strength and energy to immediately rebook my flight back home, check out of the hotel in Albuquerque, drive to the airport, return the rental car, and get on the plane. Feeling a sense of panic overwhelm me, even as I tried to focus on the immediate tasks before me, I checked out of the hotel, hopped in my rental car, and in my haste to get to the airport, backed into a car parked behind me. When I explained to the owner of the car that my wife had just been diagnosed with breast cancer and I needed to get home quickly, and as he looked over the car and saw just a scratch on the front bumper, this total stranger kindly told me to go on and expressed his hope that my wife would be okay.

The flight from Albuquerque to Denver, straight north over the mountains, was incredibly turbulent, even for a seasoned flier like me. I closed my eyes and focused on the serenity prayer, trying to find peace in accepting that which I could not change, to find courage to change that which I could (i.e., my attitude toward what I was now faced with), and the courage to know the difference. I also kept breathing deeply. Without knowing it, I was meditating and had entered an altered state of consciousness. I was at peace for the moment, despite the fear and panic that had entered my life, and despite the heavy turbulence of the flight. I actually became unaware, or at least unaffected by, the awful turbulence.

While Mark was preparing to return home, I made numerous calls. I called my mother and stepfather in Florida. Then I called my father and stepmother in town, who offered to pick up Laura from work and bring her home. I agreed, certain I couldn't do it myself. I called a couple of close friends. When I called work to say I would be out for a while, the colleague who took the message started weeping.

It wasn't long before Laura arrived. I gave her the news and it went much as expected. Laura said little, keeping her emotions in check. Finally, she looked up at me, asking, "What does this mean for Jenni and me?"

That was a hard question to answer. Did Laura want to know her own risk of getting cancer, or did she want to know if they would soon end up motherless? I shared what I knew, despite my own pain.

Eventually my parents went home and my daughters went to bed. It felt a bit lonely, but further talking about the diagnosis would not have helped at that point in time. Everyone was emotionally drained. I went to bed but could not sleep. I wanted my husband, my life partner, home. I desperately wanted to feel Mark's embrace.

It was about 5:30 in the morning when the taxi dropped Mark off at home. As he opened the door, there I stood. Our eyes said it all. We immediately embraced, held each other, felt our bodies throb with the gut-wrenching tears that flowed and flowed and flowed. We talked. I told him more about the diagnosis of a malignant tumor in my breast and the need to schedule surgery in the next week. It was unknown, at this point, whether the cancer had gone into my lymph nodes. We hoped and prayed it had not, for this would be far more serious.

In the evening, after more talk and more tears, my surgeon called. We discussed options. Lumpectomy? Mastectomy? Radiation? Chemotherapy? There were no sure-fire cures for breast cancer and no clear answers for treatment.

Over the next few days I felt my emotions surge, fade, and return. Shock. Disbelief. Terror. Fear—fear of pain, of suffering, of loss, of the unknown, of death. I felt so sad, so tired, so helpless.

But there was little anger. The disease seemed more random than personal. Instead of thinking, "Why me?" I thought, "Why not me?" After all, breast cancer affects one in eight women. It kills more women between the ages of thirty-five and fifty-four in the United States than any other disease.

Our faith in God became a source of strength. We prayed about facing the unknown, about our fear, about the need for guidance and support in making difficult choices. We put ourselves in God's hands because we knew we didn't have the strength to face the journey alone.

Hope is an orientation of the spirit, an orientation of the heart. It is not the conviction that something will turn out well, but the certainty that something makes sense, regardless of how it turns out.

– Vaclav Havel

After much prayer and discussion with Mark, I decided how I would proceed. The first step would be a lumpectomy to remove the tumor (with a lymph node resection to be sure the cancer had not spread beyond the breast area). Then, while still anesthetized, a "frozen section" would be analyzed to make sure the whole tumor had been removed. If cancer was still evident, the surgeon would perform a full mastectomy then and there. That way, another operation wouldn't be required. And perhaps after six weeks of conventional radiation treatment, I could still make the trip to Hawaii that Mark and I had planned, then I could get on with grad school. Perhaps I could handle part-time work, too, and keep some normalcy in my life. Since I had caught the cancer early and the diagnostic exams were so uncertain, I felt that the tumor was bound to be small and the lymph nodes clear.

Surgery was set for Tuesday, four days after the diagnosis.

I stopped by my workplace to visit my colleagues. I missed them; they were a touchstone, and my life had changed so much so quickly. "You look great!" they told me. They couldn't believe that I—who always ate right, exercised, and took good care of myself—had breast cancer.

I had accepted the fact that cancer was not fair. And the day before surgery, after all the preoperative blood tests and chest X-rays were done, I actually felt a bit of resolve and peace. I had never had surgery before, but reassured myself that people survived it every day.

That night I looked at my right breast, wondering if it would be gone the next day or if just a portion would be missing. This breast was part of my identity as a woman. It had nurtured my two babies. I honored the pleasure it had brought me and felt sad about the pending loss. That night in bed, I sobbed.

Treatment

We arrived at the hospital around 6:00 A.M. I went through admissions and felt pretty brave. Up in surgical prep, my strength continued. I insisted that the nurses and physicians promise to tell me immediately after the surgery what procedure had been done—I didn't want to wait till I was back in my room.

Mark, Laura, and Jenni joined my father and mother in the surgery waiting room. Surgery, they were told, would take about ninety minutes. Despite some anxiety, optimism prevailed. As Mark tells it:

Small talk punctuated long stretches of silence in the waiting room. One at a time, the minutes added up to 90. Then 100. I was counting. 120. A sense of dread rose up like a fog at sea. What could be taking so long? The nurse said an hour and a half. It had now been two. Were there complications? Did they think the cancer had spread? No! It can't be! I reviewed the facts: Alexa had taken good care of herself over the years. She was healthy. She'd discovered the mass early. There was no breast cancer in her family history that would put her at greater risk. Her mammograms were unremarkable. At worst, the cancer was highly treatable and curable.

Three-and-a-half hours and no news. Our small talk had long since been swallowed in fear.

At long last, the surgeon sent a message that she'd be coming down shortly to report on Alexa's condition. We sat in a small conference room. But even before the surgeon began to speak, I sensed my world falling apart. Speaking, training, and consulting engagements—all canceled. Classes—now covered by colleagues. All I could manage now was supporting Alexa, myself, and our daughters. Just barely. I would do the best I could to be present: to pay attention, to let in the pain and let it out as needed. When possible, to marshal my thoughts toward strength and healing.

The cancer had spread, the surgeon explained, and a mastectomy had been performed. Alexa's entire right breast was removed along with a cluster of lymph nodes from her right armpit. How much the cancer had spread would be known from the final pathology report in a couple days.

Our worst fears were confirmed. We were stunned and terrified. How could this be? Why was this happening? Time stood still. I seemed to float out of my body and over the room as the news was delivered.

In the recovery room, it was a nurse with compassionate eyes who told me, "They had to do a mastectomy." I felt I should cry, but the nurse was so gentle, and the morphine postponed my emotions. I let myself rest in the haze.

A while later, I was brought down to the ward. My family, my minister, and a best friend hovered around with anxious looks. But I was smiling, radiant. I was very glad to see my family again. Mark held my hand and let me know that whatever lay ahead, we would face it together. Laura burst into tears and I consoled her.

"Everything is going to be okay," I said to her. "The worst is over."

For the first twenty-four hours, my pain was managed pretty well with an intravenous drip. But when my physician put me on oral medication, the pain on the right side of my chest raged out of control. I told the nurse, and the nurse called the doctor; the doctor needed to see me before making a change, so I waited. I was miserable for hours. Eventually

I got angry. I didn't think I should have to suffer when I knew there were stronger medications that would help, and I resented the fact that my healthcare providers didn't trust my judgment about my experience. Finally, the doctor came by. He asked a couple of questions. I stood my ground and he prescribed a different oral pain medication. Two hours later, the pain eased up. But the time from complaint to relief took much too long.

Mark and I got the final pathology report within two days, as promised. The reporter, an oncologist we'd never met, coldly pronounced: "Infiltrating ductal carcinoma of the breast with metastatic adenocarcinoma in 50 percent of lymph nodes examined." The sentence was handed down.

What were the treatment recommendations for this stage-II cancer? Chemotherapy and a still experimental, $70,000 peripheral stem-cell transplant (not covered by insurance). This seemed like a last-ditch effort. Plus, the risks were high and the side effects horrendous. Our hope for a less extreme treatment vanished. What were the options if the transplant did not work? "None," he said.

I had worked in both a hospice and a bone marrow transplant unit, and I knew what cancer treatments did to the body. Would I have the stamina to endure it? It was hard enough already to cope with all the psychological and physical assaults—the discovery, the biopsy, the mastectomy, and now the definitive diagnosis and proposed treatment. I had read many bad "path" reports, but I never imagined my name would be on one. And yet, there it was. Alexa Umbreit. It was so foreign, so frightening, I couldn't think. And then came the notion: *I don't accept your approach, Doctor. I need a second opinion.* It gave me hope. I would get a second opinion.

•

Just two days after surgery, I came home, relieved that the surgery was over but unsure about what my future would bring. Chemotherapy? Yes. Radiation? Perhaps. But who knew what else? I felt very sad about the pain my loved ones were going through—husband, daughters, parents, other family and friends. It hurt me. But I had no energy with which to help them. In fact, I had almost no energy at all. (Was it the feelings of fear, grief, and sadness? The stress of the surgery? A combination?) Family helped a lot, but I hated feeling dependent. In fact, I felt physically handicapped. The tightness in my right arm was so painful that I could hardly move it. And since I was right-handed, every activity was a clumsy effort. I did my arm exercises faithfully, though they were tedious and improvement was slow. For weeks, the only pain-free position I could sleep in was on my back with my arm resting on pillows.

One day, I noticed a thick cord-like section in my armpit. My doctor didn't know for certain what it was, but he assured me it wasn't serious. I asked for physical therapy, but neither my family physician nor my surgeon felt it would help much. They said things like, "This may take a long time to resolve" and "You may have to live with this discomfort." I wondered what was meant by "a long time"; I wondered whether my doctor would characterize such serious pain as mere "discomfort" if he were experiencing it himself. To me, these responses seemed insensitive and controlling. I refused to accept them and insisted on giving physical therapy a chance.

And my physicians listened. I earned a referral for six physical therapy sessions to loosen up a "frozen shoulder." After the very first visit, I felt relief. It turned out that the thick cord-like section in my armpit was scar tissue along my lymph system, and it needed to be broken up with treatment and exercise in order to release the tightness. Soon, I added massage therapy to promote general relaxation as well as reduce the scar tissue. Mark learned the technique for breaking up the tissue and performed this massage therapy for me every day for months.

All this reminded me that specialists were not the only healthcare professionals who could help. And even oncologists don't know everything about the side effects of cancer treatments. In fact, some don't necessarily know the best treatment for a given diagnosis!

With this awareness, I gained a great sense of freedom. I did not need to resign myself to every recommendation made by the unknown, unfriendly oncologist. His word simply wasn't the last word. Instead, I could enlist the help of real friends—Mark, my breast cancer nurse clinician, cancer survivors I knew, and others—in deciding on treatment options and selecting a new oncologist. I prayed for help in making the best decisions. I had barely finished drawing up my list of qualifications for the ideal oncologist when my nurse clinician told me about Dr. K.

Dr. K. worked at the local research hospital. During a consultation, Dr. K. listened carefully to me and even included Mark in the deliberations. Her knowledge of breast cancer research and treatments was commanding. The stem-cell transplant, she felt, was too aggressive, expensive, and dangerous. Moreover, it was not necessarily a better form of treatment. Instead, Dr. K. proposed a four-month regimen of high-dose combination drug chemotherapy that was specific for my tumor type. Her recommendation was supported by research. She shared the published articles with us.

Research showed that the chance of no recurrence within five years was 40 to 60 percent. Mark and I both trusted and felt comfortable with Dr. K., and I chose to work with her.

Three weeks after surgery (and the day after I was accepted into graduate school), I went in for my first chemotherapy treatment. Mark was determined to take me each time and stay with me until it was over. His heart ached for me, and being present with me during the treatment was one small way to help relieve some of my suffering.

Three potent drugs were injected into a vein in my arm. Mark and I watched. Little was said. We were both too afraid; I had told him a month ago that I could handle the surgery but not the chemo.

I felt severe burning in my head and eyes that lingered for over an hour. A bad headache followed. But there was no significant nausea. As lousy as I felt, the optimist in me figured I'd get over it in a day or two. The treatment complete, Mark took me home.

Within a couple of hours, I was vomiting steadily. Frequent diarrhea followed. I tried to keep food and drink down—nutrition and fluids were very important—but I couldn't do it. I tried relaxation exercises, guided imagery, prayer—anything to stop this sick feeling—but nothing worked. Hot and cold flashes rippled through my body. I shook and grew fatigued. Except for frequent trips to the bathroom, I was confined to a chair in the living room. On the fourth day, I was hospitalized for dehydration.

The worst part of the journey had begun. The surgical pain could not compare to the impact of chemotherapy. From that point on, I was hospitalized every month for three to four days during the highest dose of my treatment cycle. Each round left me more depleted than the last, and I wondered if I would survive. My immune system was damaged and I had several bouts with infections. I lost weight and all my hair. My body ached. I suffered shortness of breath, strange sensations on my skin, and vision changes. I became hypersensitive to cold and heat, tastes and smells. My skin and mucous membranes dried up. I bled easily. I suffered massive fatigue. I could hardly remember to take the medications to control the nausea (which lasted for at least ten out of every twenty-eight days).

At this point, I said, "I look like a person who has cancer!"

I felt worthless and helpless much of the time. I couldn't manage simple household tasks, much less go back to work. I had always been a giver. But now that my body had betrayed me, I had no choice but to receive. It was hard to accept all the favors, the gifts of love from family and friends. I longed for the strength to take care of myself again.

Then came despair. I looked for some purpose in all my suffering and my family's suffering, but I found none. My optimism vanished; I didn't know how much more I could take, and I prayed regularly to regain a little control in my life.

•

Eventually I let go and surrendered to what I called God's Divine Plan. After that, support appeared "like angels." Friends wrote cards and letters and checked in by phone. They sent flowers and brought over food. As my strength improved, they began to visit me in person. My parents watched over me. My daughters drew close and gave me both physical and emotional support. Eventually, my own prayers, along with those of my family and friends, gave me a profound sense of peace. Each day I looked for something positive, if only the simple act of breathing. Each day became a gift.

I began to focus on healing and wellness. A video series called *Healing and the Mind* taught Mark and me new ways of looking at illness and treatment. After learning that humor is helpful—it releases important chemicals into the body and relieves stress—I began watching sitcoms on TV and comedies on video. I did stretching exercises regularly, which helped me regain mobility in my right arm, prevented my joints and muscles from getting too stiff, and kept my inactive body in reasonable shape.

> *It is by surmounting difficulties, not by sinking under them, that we discover our fortitude.*
>
> *– Hannah Webster Foster*

I reviewed my nursing manuals, read articles, and consulted with my doctors. Mark reviewed numerous articles and books. I collected affirmations and inspiring quotes and would refer to them when I needed a boost. I discovered complementary therapies that would come to enrich my life and Mark's. And perhaps most important, I talked about my feelings with my listeners. I learned to do whatever worked. Rest. Laugh. Exercise. Eat well. These were the basics.

•

When I was wiped out by chemo and struggling to cope, how was Mark? Where did his strength come from? How did he face the horror and helplessness of watching his spouse, his high school sweetheart, suffer the wrath of chemotherapy? The threat of death?

In periodic moments of solitude each day, I wept, sobbed. Though I wanted to deny my powerlessness and vulnerability, I did not. Though I wanted to run from the possible death of my life partner, I did not. A stronger part of me chose to let my tears wash the pain through me, over and over again. By letting myself fall apart in these moments of solitude, I managed, like Alexa, to keep myself together. I learned to accept my terror, to work with it, to make it a part of myself. Out of that darkness, strength emerged, even hope. Forced to accept the things I could not change, I learned that, with God's help, I could manage whatever lay ahead.

Housekeeping, cooking, chauffeuring the girls around, keeping family and friends up-to-date—I was now the primary parent. The hardest part was talking with

Laura and Jenni about their mom. They were afraid of losing her, and so was I. At breakfast one morning, while Alexa was in the hospital, Laura asked a question that nearly broke my heart: "Could Mom die from this?" We both knew the answer, but I wanted to offer hope for Laura as well as for myself. "Yes, Laura, women do die from breast cancer. But your mom is a strong woman and she's determined to fight this illness with all she's got." This was the truth.

With family, friends, and God, Alexa and I held on through the chemo and the fear.

Posttreatment

It had been four long months. Chemotherapy was over and I could begin to heal. But instead of feeling joy and relief, Mark and I felt unsure and afraid.

Mark worried about recurrence. Have the treatments worked? Would I have a recurrence in the months ahead? How would the family cope if I got sick again? What would the future be like?

I went through my "Now what?" phase. Now what was I supposed to do with my life? Would I regain enough energy to be productive and return to the profession I loved? If so, how long would it take? Could I ever trust my body again? Every ache and pain caused alarm. Was it cancer sneaking up again? Why couldn't medicine detect cancer at an earlier stage? Would I be alive next Christmas? My next birthday? My daughters' graduations and future weddings? And how could I protect Laura and Jenni? I couldn't plan ahead. What was the use? Why spend money on things that I might not be around to enjoy a year from now? Too often, I felt empty and sad and alone and regretful. Mark, Laura, and Jenni encouraged me to let go of the past and embrace the future. Finishing treatment was something to celebrate! Laura and Jenni eventually helped me build a new wardrobe, since I had lost quite a bit of weight, so I could feel pretty again. I hadn't felt feminine, let alone pretty, in many months.

My energy started to come back, but progress was slow. It would take months to build up the stamina to return to work. Still, I felt good just being able to drive a car or go on an errand alone. I had felt overprotected, even smothered at times, by the well-intentioned people who loved me. I longed for independence, for normal activity in my life.

Cancer is so limited ...
It cannot cripple love
It cannot shatter hope
It cannot corrode faith
It cannot eat away peace
It cannot destroy confidence
It cannot kill friendship
It cannot shut out memories
It cannot invade the soul
It cannot reduce eternal life
It cannot quench the spirit
It cannot lessen the power of the resurrection

– Anonymous

Six weeks after my last chemo treatment, our postponed wish for a vacation in Hawaii, with just Mark and I together, came true. Despite the unknowns, we were able to rejoice and recuperate together under a tropical sun. It was in Hawaii where I realized the importance that nature plays in the healing process. There my body began to restore itself, and a new "normal" began to emerge.

Reintegration

It was a big day when I reached the first anniversary of my cancer diagnosis. Since my birthday fell in the same month, the family celebrated both events. I no longer dreaded growing older, but rejoiced in my health and longevity. The fatigue was gone and I was working as a nurse again. Reintegration had begun, and the "gifts of cancer," as ironic as it seems, were becoming clearer.

I now saw that my simple purpose in life was to learn, to grow, and to share love. I felt deeply grateful for each day's many blessings, especially for family and for those whose love and support helped me survive my illness. I learned that I had little control over much of what happened to my body. For example, while I could control how I cared for my body and how I reacted to stress, I could not control the things that caused my stress. After meeting other cancer survivors—people who understood one another so well, they could talk about anything—I learned to identify my fears and to release them. As a result, fear no longer dominated my life.

Living with cancer is a catalyst,
an opportunity for reevaluation,
insight, and change.
This is not to say that we don't also have negative
and frightening thoughts and that we don't
sometimes feel overwhelmed by the fear
of recurrence and the fear of death.
Do we deny them?
Do we hold back what we truly feel?
The answer, of course, is no.
But we transpose the tragedy of what has happened to us
into something positive ...
It is within my power to turn fear into a positive opportunity!

– Linda Dackman

As my fear diminished, my focus on disease diminished, too. I began to support my healing process in earnest. I practiced life-giving activities and spent more time nurturing myself. For example, I read books on mind-body therapies and spirituality, as did Mark. I attended retreats on women and spirituality. When I felt a surge of anxiety, I read my notebook of affirmations, sang calming songs to myself, or used guided imagery, often with Mark, or prayer to get centered again. I developed the freedom to say no: "No, I don't want to" and "No, I can't." To ease stress and release toxins, I paid more attention to deep breathing throughout the day. Because I lacked my former stamina, I learned to give myself permission to rest. And though I experienced more aches and pains than before, I learned to cope.

It seemed to me that whenever I got stuck or had a yearning, someone would come along and offer exactly what I needed. I called these people my "angels," and all I needed to do was pay attention to their arrival and guidance. Support groups reassured me that many others had been on a similar path and that they, too, were surviving. I began to focus on living in the present moment, on just being. If it wasn't life-threatening, it wasn't worth getting upset over, for both Mark and me. Without realizing it, we had changed our view of life. True, I wasn't exactly grateful to have had cancer, and I would not have wished it on anyone, but Mark and I were certain it had improved our lives and made us better people.

I began to hope that my body might not let me down again—at least for a while—and that I might celebrate more anniversaries with Mark and see my children graduate from college. I thought about being around for the millennium.

Hope reigns in my life today
My illness does not rule me
Daily I seek to
Acknowledge the physical,
Be positive in the mental,
Transcend the emotional,
Anchor in the spiritual,
Knowing that God's peace is my goal.
Thank you, Lord, for today's blessing!

– The Triumphant Patient's Creed

With this renewed sense of self and emerging hope, I set out to learn as much as I could. I realized how fragile, how short life is, and I felt a responsibility to learn more in order to serve others better. After a seven-month delay, I felt strong enough to return to graduate school. Four-and-a-half years later, I graduated with a master's degree in nursing—and a 4.0 GPA. I was proud of this accomplishment, but more than that, I was proud of having survived cancer!

·

It has been several years since Mark and I confronted illness and death so directly. We firmly believe that, despite our fear, pain, and uncertainty, the experience has enriched our lives. Relationships have deepened and priorities have become clearer. It's a paradox: when our hearts and minds are open, and when we let go of the illusion of control, our suffering can bring spiritual gifts of awareness and acceptance. Here are some of the gifts that Mark and I received—lessons that we learned:

All things pass.

By letting go, one can enjoy the present.

When fears are named and analyzed, their power fades.

Death need not be feared; it is as natural as the changing of the seasons.

Each day of good health is a blessing.

Each day of meaningful work is a blessing.

Each day of loving relationships is a blessing.

Nature is a gift that can balance and refresh the spirit.

When priorities are clear, wants and needs
become simpler.

When life is lived as a prayer and in service to one
another (and oneself), inner peace blossoms.

Today my goal is to live each day with hope, compassion, and joy. Although impatient at times with my progress, I remind myself to focus on the journey, not the destination. That's where the real teachings lie.

CHAPTER TWO

Pathways to Healing

During the initial months following my cancer diagnosis, the support of family and friends was very soothing. It also helped that my oncologist was responsive to Mark's and my input in choosing my treatment. Yet, a feeling of powerlessness lingered. My future seemed to depend on others, particularly on medical professionals.

Then we were introduced to several therapeutic techniques that enabled us to participate in our own healing, both as individuals and as a couple. This began a process of transformation: we learned to live in the present moment with a renewed passion for life, and we no longer felt powerless. We gained a growing recognition of the preciousness of life, of our inner strength, and of the many gifts of the spirit available to all of us. As we learned more about the mind-body connection and various complementary healing modalities, our lives truly became enriched. We began to look at life with new eyes and to regularly tap into what Herbert Benson has described as the "relaxation response" in order to manage stress and maintain wellness.

> *Look to this day, for it is life.*
> *For yesterday is already a dream*
> *and tomorrow is only a vision.*
> *But today, well lived,*
> *makes every yesterday a dream of happiness,*
> *and every tomorrow a vision of hope.*
>
> *— Sanskrit proverb*

Mark and I were not predisposed to alternative or complementary healing techniques, nor did we subscribe to New Age philosophies. In fact, we continue to be skeptical of the simplistic self-healing advice that is frequently offered by self-help books and New Age teachers in Western culture. On the other hand, we have learned to deeply respect the ageless wisdom of the traditions and cultures upon which many New Age practices are based. Powerful healing often occurs in these traditions, even though they may seem foreign to our own belief systems.

When Mark and I began to explore complementary therapies, we embarked on a remarkable journey, one that has deepened our relationship and led to more balanced, less stressful lives. We share what we have learned in order to give you a starting point for your own journey, whether you or your loved one are struggling with a serious illness, grief, or stress. What we offer here is not meant to be prescriptive, but to give you an idea of the many healing options worth exploring.

Suggested Guidelines for Healing

Each person's journey toward strength and healing is unique. The most important thing is having the courage to find resources that help us tap into our inner wisdom to guide our choices and identify our preferences for promoting wellness. We must use what works for us, surrounding ourselves with that which is sustaining and avoiding anything that is depleting.

First of all, I needed to determine what healing meant to me. Did healing mean total cure, erasing what I had experienced over the past few months, or eliminating feelings of powerlessness and fear? What was realistic, given my circumstances? I opened my mind to new definitions of healing, which did not necessarily mean finding a cure. Gerald Jampolsky spoke of "health as inner peace and healing as letting go of fear." Deepak Chopra wrote, "Health is not just the absence of disease. It's an inner joyfulness that should be ours all the time—a state of positive well being." One of the most powerful definitions of healing that I found came from *Rituals of Healing* by Jeanne Achterberg, Barbara Dossey, and Leslie Kolkmeier:

Healing is:

A lifelong journey into wholeness

Seeking harmony and balance in one's own life, in
family, community, and global relations

An instant of transcendence—above and beyond the self

Embracing what is most feared

Opening what has been closed, softening what has
been hardened into obstruction

Creativity and passion and love

Seeking and expressing self in its fullness; its light
and shadow, its male and female

Remembering what has been forgotten about
connection, and unity, and interdependence among
all things living and nonliving

Learning to trust life

When we look at healing in this manner, we gain a whole
new perspective. We realize that healing and wellness are part
of a lifelong journey, rather than something we can attain
through surgery, drugs, or other treatments. Healing not only
promotes wholeness, integrating all parts of the self, but also
provides hope, teaching us to trust life. Healing allows us to
embrace and transform what is frightening or painful in life.
This was what I was seeking.

Mark and I found much of our healing journey reflected in
the words of Achterberg, Dossey, and Kolkmeier. We combined
many of their suggestions with the wisdom of our other teachers to create a guide to beginning your own healing journey:

- *Find a place of solitude and go there daily. You* might seek out a favorite chair in your favorite room, the shady spot under an old tree, a quiet park, a sacred mountain, or the edge of a river. Let this be your special place, a place of reflection where the power of silence will cleanse your soul.

- *Reflect on the meaning of your diagnosis or treatment.* What are your priorities now? How will life change? What are your reasons for staying alive? Use this time to gain strength and perspective. Remember, few problems advance so quickly that you must rush into making decisions.

- *Be gentle with yourself, and look for balance in* your daily life. Surround yourself with all that is nurturing and life-giving. Learn to say no, and avoid negative people. Focus on what is important in your life, and put your energy there. This is especially important when life has become tumultuous after a frightening diagnosis.

- *Write in a journal or talk with a trusted friend. This* can help to flush out your thoughts and release your emotions, which is cleansing for the mind.

- *Spend time in prayer or surrounded by nature (which* also promotes a quiet, prayerful state). Studies show that prayer can help with healing.

- *Find at least one person—a friend, counselor, or* advocate—who can be your primary support person.

When you think you are going crazy, when you are sure you are doomed, when your head is buzzing with uncertainty, you can rely on this person to listen and offer encouragement.

- *Gather information about your disease and options* for treatment. Keep an open mind, but understand that anyone who offers advice may have something to gain by it. It's okay to seek second and third opinions from healthcare professionals.

- *Explore complementary therapies that help you* focus on healing, decrease tension, and maintain inner peace. When you achieve a more relaxed state, your body is better able to heal. Relaxation causes chemical reactions to occur in the body, promoting healing and restoration.

- *Take command of your healthcare team. Healthcare* professionals are performing a service for you, and you are paying their salaries. Make sure they communicate with each other, and never let anyone talk you into a test or treatment that you don't believe in or don't understand. Ask questions, and replace anyone who seems too busy to give you the answers you need. Remember, you hired them, and you can fire them.

- *Know that gentleness and compassion can be taught* to the most arrogant doctor and the crankiest nurse. Kindly tell them what you need. If they cannot handle it, find someone else who can.

- *Keep these important facts in mind:*
  - Sometimes, bad things happen to good people.
  - When people get sick, there is often no simple reason why.
  - Everything cures somebody, and nothing cures everybody.

- *Collect positive affirmations and reread them daily.* This can help you stay focused on healing. Books can be inspirational, too, such as Bernie Siegel's *Love, Medicine, and Miracles,* which describes the characteristics of exceptional patients who survived against all odds.

- *Join a survivor support group, where no question is ever deemed "silly."* Survivor groups can provide a reliable network of understanding, affirming support persons. In fact, studies have shown an increased length of survivorship among those who participate in survivor support groups.

God grant me the serenity to accept the things
I cannot change, the courage to change the things
I can, and the wisdom to know the difference.

— Reinhold Niebuhr

In the following pages, we will explain some of the techniques, practices, and lessons that we found to be particularly effective. Many of these techniques can be used by the support person both to reduce his or her own stress and enhance the loved one's healing process. Mark and I have integrated all of these practices into our own lives, and this has led to more balance, hope, and peace in the midst of periodic stress and grief.

Massage

After the first month of chemotherapy, I realized that I needed assistance to keep my body in the best state for healing and to receive the benefits of the chemotherapy. I had tried distraction as well as relaxation breathing exercises during severe chemotherapy reactions, but I found they were not effective in managing my multiple symptoms. So, I discussed my concerns with one of my good friends and support persons, Mary Ann. Mary Ann insisted that I make an appointment with Vi, a skilled massage therapist. This referral was one of the greatest gifts that Mary Ann gave to me. Since then, Vi has provided over six years of therapy with her healing hands to me and my family.

In addition to this gift, Mary Ann taught me several very difficult lessons. Less than a week after she had introduced me to the positive benefits of massage, Mark and I received news that she had died unexpectedly and suddenly in her sleep from a brain aneurysm. We were in a state of shock. How could this happen to our healthy friend and support person? It was my life that had been threatened, not Mary Ann's! The only way to make sense out of this was to realize that the hour of our death is not known. Rather than worry about tomorrow, we should live each day as if it is our last. To think that we can predict our future is an illusion that may very well be shattered as destiny unfolds. These lessons were a turning point in my views on life and death.

Mary Ann's gift of massage was another turning point for me. Massage is the use of the hands to apply pressure and movement on the skin and underlying muscle. Its purpose is to enhance physical and psychological relaxation, improve circulation of the blood and lymph systems, relieve sore muscles, stimulate weak muscles, improve skin function, and stimulate the autonomic nervous system (which is responsible for all bodily functions). Massage helps to keep the body in a greater sense of balance, promoting optimum health.

There are many kinds of massage:

- *Swedish massage* is a vigorous technique that uses long, smooth strokes on the skin, kneading and patting on the muscles, and circular movements on the joints. Its primary benefits are relaxation and improved blood and lymph circulation.

- *Esalen massage* uses long, smooth strokes with a light touch to promote relaxation.

- *Reflexology* is a deep foot and hand massage using pressure and stroking. It is based on the assumption that there are specific points on the feet and hands which correspond to organs in the body. By massaging these areas, a release of tension or energy blockages occur in those organs.

- *Shiatsu* comes from a Japanese tradition and uses pressure points to release energy blockages along the meridian energy system in the body. Shiatsu is helpful in relieving stress. *Acupressure* (from Chinese tradition) and *jin shin jitsu* (another variation of a pressure point therapy) are similar to shiatsu.

- *Tui na* is a traditional Chinese massage that also focuses on removing obstructions in the energy pathways of the body. It promotes an increase in the body's vital energy.

Choosing a massage therapist, like choosing a physician, may take some research. Ask friends and acquaintances for referrals. Call therapists to ask if they have experience treating clients with your illness and if they are confident that they can help you. You will want someone with years of experience. If the therapist attended a school that was licensed by your state and accredited by a major organization, such as the American Massage Therapy Association, this is a good credential.

Massages can range from $40 to $90 an hour depending on where you live. Your therapist can recommend how often you need a massage. Once you've had a few sessions, you will recognize how your body feels at rest—this is the perfect healing state. Then you'll be able to recognize when your muscles tense up or your body begins to ache. The key is to get another treatment before your muscles tense up too much. During chemotherapy treatment, I had a massage every one to two weeks; after chemotherapy I went every three to four weeks.

As every reputable massage therapist knows, a few precautions need to be observed when considering massage therapy. Massage should never be used near cancer sites or open wounds, or in the presence of fever, infection, jaundice, hemorrhaging, a blood clot, or inflamed blood vessels. Also, certain health conditions require very gentle massage, so you should always inform your therapist of your illness.

Be sure to inform your physician that you are receiving massage as part of your treatment. As long as the precautions are followed, most healthcare providers will support this therapy if it makes the patient feel better.

Guided Imagery

In the search for other methods to help in the healing process, Mark and I read about guided imagery. We learned that guided imagery can help initiate relaxation, ease pain, assist in wound healing, aid the birthing process, stabilize vital signs, support grieving, and it has even been postulated to boost immune system function and fight cancer cells. It was worth a try. Mark and I were fortunate to have a friend, Kathy, who had worked for a physician who used guided imagery extensively. After Kathy brought us an audiotape series called *Healing Yourself* by Martin Rossman, MD, our serious practice began.

Guided imagery is the use of the imagination to gain insight, alter perceptions, and redirect physiology. It can serve as a bridge connecting the body, mind, and spirit. Those who practice guided imagery will use their mind to form an image that involves one or more of the senses. The image, which has a personal healing significance, is directed to the body part or activity requiring attention.

This technique requires a guide, whether a professional therapist (on audiotape, videotape, or in the room with you) or an internal, spiritual guide (a wise person, God, a "universal power," or a spirit) that emerges at some point during an imagery experience.

There are multiple audiotapes and videotapes available to assist with guided imagery, and professionally trained therapists will often make individual tapes for specific needs. It is important to find a voice that soothes you. Ideally, your own image of healing will arise after only a few suggestions from your guide. If the guide suggests an image that feels too prescriptive and detailed, it may not be meaningful to you. Trust the image your mind prefers to create; it will be what you need at that moment. There is no right or best image, so simply relax and remain open to the image that arises.

Imagery involves the skillful use of imagination, which affects the psyche in complex ways. Generally, persons with psychoses should avoid guided imagery. People who have fundamental spiritual beliefs that prevent deep introspection also may want to avoid this technique. Those who have experienced deep psychological, physical, or sexual trauma should only use imagery under the supervision of a trained professional, such as a psychologist, psychiatrist, physician, social worker, nurse, or chaplain. Be sure to ask about a professional's training and credentials before using his or her services.

Healing Touch

Healing Touch energy therapy was another gift that presented itself to me at just the right time and place. Our friend Kathy had recommended that I check out a local organization that offered free support services to those facing life-threatening illnesses, chronic illnesses, or grief and loss issues. It was my intent to access a massage session, but there were no openings. However, there was a Healing Touch session open with a nurse named Mary. It sounded interesting, and I figured would do no harm, so I went.

Mary was a gentle, nurturing "angel" who worked with her hands in the "energy field" above my body. She used only the lightest touch on my body to bring about total relaxation and a feeling of balance and peace that I had never before experienced. I felt exactly where Mary's hands were at all times, even with my eyes closed. After the session had ended, Mary and I talked at length about written resources describing Healing Touch and other mind-body therapies. I promised myself that when I was well, I would learn this fascinating technique to use with patients in my professional nursing practice.

Healing Touch therapy uses hands-on and energy-based techniques to balance and align the human energy field, influencing health at the physical, emotional, mental, and spiritual levels. It blends a number of techniques, both ancient and contemporary. Healing Touch is based on the belief that human beings are composed of layers of energy. This may sound far-fetched; however, our body's internal energy is measured by electrocardiograms, brain wave tests, and magnetic resonance diagnostic machines. Humans can perceive light and sound, which are simply patterns of energy. And scientists have developed instruments that can measure an individual's bio-magnetic field. When someone is ill or in distress, the pattern and organization of his or her energy field is disrupted. Skilled practitioners can sense this disruption and use their hands to rebalance the energy.

Many of the underlying principles and practices of Healing Touch are found in numerous ancient cultural and religious traditions, such as the "laying on of hands" in Christian tradition, reiki in Japan, ayurveda in India, qigong in China, and energy-based healing from Native American culture.

Healing Touch is effective in managing pain, reducing anxiety, speeding postoperative recovery, enhancing the immune system, reducing depression, and promoting a sense of well being. While Healing Touch is not curative, it complements conventional medical care.

Practitioners attend a rigorous, multilevel training program to become adept at their work. Before choosing a practitioner, be sure to inquire about his or her level of training and experience.

There are no known side effects of Healing Touch therapy, but the very young, very old, and extremely ill require gentle treatments, as they tend to be more sensitive to energy work. When a person has cancer, Healing Touch should not concentrate on a particular area, but should balance the entire energy field.

Prayer and Meditation

Prayer has always been an important part of our lives. Typically our prayers have expressed absolute gratitude for abundant blessings or petitions to help those in need. However, when I was the one in need and the crisis was intense, my prayers were not easily stated.

I learned that prayer can simply be a cry of anguish, an appeal for help in getting through a crisis. The words are not important, only the feeling in the heart. Larry Dossey describes prayer as "communication with the Absolute." Whether it comes from yourself or from others, prayer is a powerful healing practice. It promotes inner peace by tapping into deeply personal beliefs, whether religious or philosophic. The beauty of prayer is that anyone can use it any time and any place. It can take the form of words, music, creation, motion, stillness, even the appreciation of a child at play. A prayer is anything that brings you in contact with the Divine.

After my cancer diagnosis, we spent a great deal of time in prayer and meditation. Simply stated, meditation is the act of achieving relaxation and inner peace by creating a quiet space and keeping your attention pleasantly anchored in the present moment. Meditation, common to all religious and spiritual traditions, teaches you the profound benefits of just sitting still. It requires practice, concentration, and discipline. We learned meditation through reading, attending workshops, and practice, practice, practice.

The Lord is my pacesetter, I shall not rush;
He makes me stop and rest.
He offers me images of stillness;
He gives me calmness of mind,
And His guidance is peace.
Even though I have many things to accomplish,
I will not fret, for He is near.
He will keep me in balance.
He refreshes and renews me in the midst of activity
He anoints my mind with oils of tranquility.
My cup of joyful energy runs over.
Surely serenity and harmony shall fill my days,
For I shall walk with the Lord and dwell within
Him forever.

– Japanese version of Psalm 23

A particularly helpful and easy-to-learn form of meditation is the Buddhist practice of mindfulness. In *Wherever You Go There You Are,* meditation teacher Jon Kabat-Zinn calls mindfulness a simple concept. "Its power lies in its practice and its application. Mindfulness means paying attention in a particular way: on purpose, in the present moment, and nonjudgmentally. This kind of attention nurtures greater awareness, clarity, and acceptance of present-moment reality. . . . Mindfulness provides a simple but powerful route for getting ourselves unstuck, back into touch with our own wisdom and vitality. . . . It is the direct opposite of taking life for granted."

In the next chapter we will introduce you to "centering prayer," another form of meditation that we have integrated into our lives. Centering prayer is deeply grounded in the practices of the early Christian church and has been reintroduced to the contemporary world. For many people of many faiths, it represents an easy-to-learn, yet powerful, form of meditative practice.

Yoga, Qigong, and Tai Chi

While exercise is a powerful therapy, serious illness can make typical exercise difficult, if not impossible. Fortunately, gentle motions from Eastern healing traditions can enhance overall health.

Yoga, which comes from the Hindu tradition, involves stretching and breathing exercises, progressive deep-relaxation, and intense concentration. Its purpose is to improve flexibility and to prepare the body and mind for meditation. Qigong and tai chi come from the Chinese tradition and involve a series of dance-like movements linked in a slow, smooth sequence. Like yoga, they require strength, breath work, relaxation, and concentration.

All three techniques focus on self-awareness, well-being, and energy flow. They are based on the belief that the body's vital energy force can be cultivated. The exercises are done to move that vital energy force smoothly through your body, reducing joint pain and improving balance, posture, and circulation. These exercises can also prepare you for meditation.

> *May we all be at peace. May our hearts be*
> *open to experiencing the mystery and majesty*
> *of the precious gift of life. May we come to*
> *embrace the beauty and strength within our-*
> *selves and others. May the wounds that we*
> *carry in our souls be healed. As peacemakers,*
> *may we all become a source of healing for all*
> *those who cross our path in the journey of life.*
>
> *– Buddhist loving-kindness meditation,*
> *modified by Mark Umbreit*

Most adults do not require a healthcare screening before starting these exercise therapies; however, if you have a chronic disease (or risk factors for such a disease), be sure to consult your physician before beginning any exercise program. To help you get started, a number of communities offer yoga, qigong, and tai chi classes. Videotapes are also available.

Nutrition

The foods you put into your body will have a direct influence on healing. It does little good to pursue complementary therapies if you pollute your body with nonnutritious foods or with preservatives, pesticides, and other potential toxins. Pesticides and herbicides adversely affect the body's defense system, making it difficult to fight off toxins and carcinogens. Try to eat organic foods (foods not tainted with pesticides and herbicides). Your body may be better able to heal when it is not constantly bombarded with foods containing harmful chemicals.

To get the nutrients you need to support healthy biological functioning, you must plan a carefully constructed diet, and you may want to include supplements. I take a daily vitamin and mineral supplement containing calcium, magnesium, vitamin E, vitamin C, and a B complex. In addition, I have increased my soy protein, limited my fat intake, and drastically reduced my consumption of white flour and refined sugar.

My diet changed dramatically after Mark and I began to read about nutrition. We recommend *Cancer Survivor's Nutrition and Health Guide,* by Spiller and Bruce; *Prescription for Nutritional Healing,* by Balch and Balch; "Nutrition Action Health Letter," published monthly by the Center for Science in the Public Interest; and *Definitive Guide to Cancer,* by Diamond, Cowden, and Goldberg, which contains a chapter titled "Nutrition as Cancer Medicine: A Complete Guide to Dietary Changes and Anticancer Nutritional Supplements."

Of course, dietary needs will vary from person to person, so be sure to discuss your nutritional requirements with a professional. This will help you avoid confusing and even contradictory information.

NUTRIENT DEFICIENCIES

Studies have shown that two-thirds of the average American diet consists of fats and refined sugars, which have little or no nutritional value. Since nutrient deficiencies can weaken your body's immune defenses and make you more vulnerable to stress and illness, it's a good idea to identify the nutrients in the foods you eat. You might start by reading food labels, and perhaps buying a book on nutrition. It may take some practice, but you can plan your diet (and use specific supplements) to get the nutrients you need for healthy biological functioning. Here are some tips:

- *Try to eat foods derived from plant sources. These* are richer in nutrients and antioxidants than foods that come from animal sources.

- *Limit your consumption of fat to between 15 and 30* percent of your total caloric intake. Eat as little saturated fat as possible (found in dairy items and fatty meats such as beef, veal, lamb, pork, and ham). Avoid "transfatty" acids (artificially prepared fats) such as hydrogenated oils found in shortening, some margarines, and many commercially baked goods.

- *Red meat, if eaten at all, should be limited to less* than three ounces per day. Fish and poultry are better sources of protein.

- *Minimize your intake of alcohol and caffeine, and* drink at least six glasses of pure water per day.

A BALANCED DIET

Never overindulge in one food group while depriving yourself of another. A body in the process of healing needs a balanced diet, one that is rich in vegetables, fruits, whole grains, beans, and protein. A vegetarian diet of fruits, vegetables, beans, and grains offers two benefits: it burdens the body with fewer toxins and supports the body's anticancer defenses. It provides many antioxidants including vitamin C, beta-carotene, vitamin E, and other phytochemicals that fight cancer and "environmental" diseases.

While it's important to limit your fat consumption, minimize saturated fats, and avoid transfatty acids, remember that not all fats are bad. Grains contain "good" fats, as do soy products. Other safe fats are found in nuts (almonds, walnuts, hazelnuts), seeds (sesame, sunflower, pumpkin), some vegetables (avocados, olives), and oils derived from these foods (extra virgin olive oil or unrefined sesame oil). Research shows that monounsaturated fats (found in canola oil and olive oil) do not increase the risk of cancer, and omega-3 fatty acids (found in fish oils, flaxseed, and cold water fish such as salmon) may even have a protective effect if eaten periodically.

It's not easy to change your eating habits; in fact, it's very hard. But with patience and resolve, you can do it. Take the time to evaluate your body's needs and see if you can come up with a reasonable set of adjustments. As always, be gentle and patient with yourself. Just practice. Experiment. There are benefits in merely trying.

Music

It was during my chemotherapy reactions that Mark and I began using music to promote relaxation. We have used a variety of selections over the years and find that those with gentle nature sounds in the background are particularly sooth-ing. This practice has become a regular part of our daily lives. Each night, we go to sleep with a cassette playing gentle music and sounds of nature.

Music can affect emotions, behavior, and even physiology. It can quiet restless thinking, promote relaxation, and bring on sleep. When used on a regular basis, music can be a corner-stone in the healing journey.

The key to music therapy is finding pieces that move you into a state of deep relaxation, which promotes healing. For some, human compositions work best; for others, nature's music—gentle rain or waves, babbling brooks, or softly singing birds—is more soothing. Pay attention to the way you feel when you hear a particular piece of music. Does your breathing slow down? Do you feel peaceful or uplifted? If so, then you've found a piece that you can use in your music ther-apy. When relaxing with music, remember to start out by tak-ing a deep breath and closing your eyes. Then, let the music carry you to a tranquil place.

•

We encourage you to look beyond the practices described in this chapter and open yourself to additional pathways to heal-ing, strength, and peace. These therapies and spiritual prac-tices offer powerful and consistently effective tools to manage stress and promote healing and wellness. They can contribute to a balanced and joyful life anchored in gratitude, humility, and compassion. However, just as they do not cure, neither do they guarantee peace and joy. Stress will catch up with you now and then, and life will sometimes feel out of balance.

Mark and I continue to experience periodic stress, to feel out of balance, and to get caught up in the busyness of life. Incorporating these healing practices into a daily routine is an ongoing process. While it requires consistent effort over a long period of time, the rewards are worth it.

CHAPTER THREE

Pathways to Spirituality

For many people in Western culture, spirituality is synonymous with religion. Some regard spirituality as preachy and judgmental, particularly if they feel alienated from structured religion. Others embrace an entirely different meaning of spirituality, whether or not they belong to a well-established faith tradition.

Rachel Naomi Remen, a compassionate physician who works with cancer patients, speaks of how the spiritual is "profoundly nonjudgmental and nonseparative." It is a deep yearning for meaning and connectedness that is an essential need of human nature. Dr. Remen speaks of how this yearning varies from person to person, but is always present in each of us. It is this spiritual dimension that makes healing possible.

For her, religion is often a bridge to the spiritual, but the spiritual lies far beyond the dogmatic and judgmental tone of most religions. "Unfortunately," she adds, "in seeking the spiritual, we may become attached to the bridge rather than crossing over it."

Martha Highfield, a nurse practitioner and researcher, defines spirituality as "the human capacity to transcend self, which is reflected in three basic spiritual needs: (a) the need for self-acceptance, [characterized by] a trusting relationship with self based on a sense of meaning and purpose in life; (b) the need for relationships with others and/or a supreme other (e.g., God) characterized by unconditional love, trust, and forgiveness, and (c) the need for hope, which is the need to imagine and participate in the enhancement of a positive future." She believes that all persons experience these spiritual needs, whether or not they are part of a formal religious organization.

Health is inner peace
Healing is letting go of fear.
Love is an experience beyond definition—
    as difficult to define as God is.
Love is unconditional and never ceases.
It never judges, and it is the timeless answer
    to every problem, every sickness, and every pain.
Surrendering to love, surrendering to God, is what life
    is all about.
So I do my best to make each moment a prayer on my
    path way home to God.

        – Gerald G. Jampolsky, MD

At its core, spirituality represents a recognition of the connectedness of all human beings. It is the act of embracing and honoring life's sacred gifts: the beauty of creation, the joy of relationships, the wisdom found in diverse cultures and faith systems, and the compassion for all who cross your path.

While a serious illness or loss can do unmistakable damage to your body, the harm to your spirituality can be equally devastating, though perhaps less evident. To help you discover or rebuild the path to your spiritual life, we will present gems of wisdom from a number of spiritual traditions. We offer these pathways with deep respect for the core wisdom found in nearly all of the world religions and many secular traditions as well. But first, we'd like to discuss one of the most powerful pathways to spirituality: service to others.

We do no great things;
we do only small things, with great love.
— Mother Teresa

Service

By serving others, we come face-to-face with the sacred quality of life and relationships. Most often, service comes out of our own woundedness, not just our skills or expertise. When we serve, we become not only vulnerable, but also enriched. As Rachel Naomi Remen points out, we cannot serve from a distance. We can only serve that which we are willing to touch, that to which we are profoundly connected. This was

Mother Teresa's message, that we serve life not because it is broken, but because it is holy.

In our own family, service means many things. Over the years Mark and I have served the homeless in an inner-city shelter, helped to organize the first hospice program in our community, and volunteered for Habitat for Humanity.

We offer Healing Touch and massage to family, friends, and patients during times of stress, illness, catastrophe, and sometimes during the dying process. In all of these cases, Healing Touch brings peace and relaxation, helping the recipients to cope with difficult life challenges.

Mark volunteers weekly to support, hold, and play with kids with cancer and other serious illnesses. In addition, he periodically serves both prisoners and victims of severe violence (including parents of murdered children), offering support, a listening ear, and assistance in their journey toward healing.

Some of these services are done through volunteer work, others intersect with our careers. As a nurse, for example, I try to serve my patients by being fully present, listening with compassion as they express their needs, their fears, and their life stories.

Frankly, we are not sure who benefits the most from our service. Helping those who are different from us or who have experienced trauma or injustice—and doing so in a spirit of compassion and humility, rather than achievement and pride—is remarkably rewarding. In the words of Rachel Naomi Remen, "When you serve the life around you, you strengthen the life within you." Service to others is reciprocal. It helps keep life in perspective and can offer a lesson in humility. There are many ways to serve others; the important thing is to integrate service into the fabric of our lives. In fact, thousands of people throughout North America and abroad volunteer regularly to serve others.

To laugh often and much;
to win the respect of intelligent
*   people and affection of children;*
to earn the appreciation of honest critics and endure
*   the betrayal of false friends;*
to appreciate beauty, to find the best in others;
to leave the world a bit better, whether by a healthy child,
*   a garden patch or a redeemed social condition;*
to know even one life has breathed easier because
*   you have lived.*
This is to have succeeded.

– Ralph Waldo Emerson

Jewels of Wisdom from World Religions

For some people, the thought of different pathways to spirituality is enormously threatening and offensive. There is only one way—their way. All other traditions are viewed as heresy or superstition. It is difficult for them to consider how their own religion may be enhanced by the wisdom, beauty, and inspiration of other traditions.

Increasingly, however, people who remain deeply rooted in their own religion are becoming more open to other traditions. They are finding that the wisdom of various traditions brings new meaning and clarity to their own.

As we explore the wisdom of spiritual traditions around the world, we acknowledge that no single religion or philosophy carries the full truth, and people of all faiths have demonstrated a capacity for arrogance, intimidation, and violence. Therefore, we will ignore religious dogma and focus only on that which touches the heart and enhances healing.

The Dalai Lama, the spiritual leader of Tibetan Buddhists, offers this thought to the many disenchanted Christians who are flocking to Buddhism: There is no need to become a Buddhist. If you are a Christian, you can embrace the beauty and wisdom of Jesus while enriching your tradition through the contemplative and spiritual practices of Buddhism. Thich Nhat Hanh, a Vietnamese Zen Buddhist master, echoes this idea. He notes that the Buddha respected people's desire to maintain their own faith while learning from the practices of Buddhist mindfulness and meditation. The Buddha emphasized the need to preserve our Jewish, Christian, or Muslim roots, for that is the way to continue the Buddha nature. Cutting ourselves off from our roots can lead to unhappiness.

Mark and I are practicing Christians who have always been actively involved in church life and social justice. While we value our faith community, we hunger for a deeper experience of spirituality. Exploring the spiritual gifts from other traditions has helped us connect more deeply with the beauty and wisdom in our own religion.

The more we are exposed to the spiritual wisdom of Native American cultures, Buddhism, Taoism, Judaism, Islam, and other paths, the more we come to embrace the richness of our own tradition as nonexclusivist Christians.

We have integrated Buddhist mindfulness and meditation into our daily Christian prayers, and we practice qigong, from Taoist tradition, every day as part of our morning prayer and meditation ritual.

In the pages that follow, we will share the insight and strength we have gained from our Christian heritage, focusing on the spiritual impact rather than the formal dogma and rituals of the institutional church. We will then share beautiful and inspiring teachings from traditions other than our own—teachings from Judaism, Islam, Native American cultures, Buddhism, Hinduism, and Taoism that have enriched our lives and provided powerful spiritual guidance. By reflecting on the wisdom of these meditations and the commonalities they share, you may find that they can deepen your own spiritual journey, as well. Finally, we conclude with specific guidelines for finding your own pathway to spirituality and peace.

At the start of this new century, it is vital for world peace that we come to better understand each other's cultural and religious traditions. Mark and I share these bits of wisdom from diverse traditions in the hope that they will touch you as they have us. Rather than pull you away from your spiritual heritage, these gems may enrich your journey while allowing you to stay grounded in the core wisdom of your own tradition, whether religious or secular.

CHRISTIAN TRADITION

Mark and I have been actively involved in the Christian church since early childhood. For this reason, we provide far more background on Christianity than on other spiritual traditions.

All that we are today—all our beliefs and values—is an outgrowth of our Christian faith and tradition.

Jesus' radical and challenging words in the Sermon on the Mount and numerous other scriptures have had a profound effect on our lives. We are drawn less to the intricate Christian belief systems than to the essence of Jesus' life and ministry, his message of compassion and justice and humility, concepts which are also found in many other religions.

Our passion for honoring the richness of diverse cultures and respecting the enormous strength and capacity that we all have as children of God, regardless of our individual or collective "brokenness," is grounded in our understanding of the life-affirming and inclusive teachings of Jesus. In his ministry to criminals, prostitutes, tax collectors, and others whom "respected" religious leaders of his day refused to associate with, Jesus taught that authentic spirituality is nonjudgmental. Therefore, we believe that embracing the beauty and wisdom in other traditions in no way diminishes the beauty of our own tradition.

Our story, our Christian witness, is precisely that: our intimate and intensely lived experience that takes place in the presence of God's love. It is our encounter with the beauty and mystery of this precious and fragile gift of life we are given by the Creator. Our story does not have to cancel out your story. You may have your own deeply moving story of inspiration and faith within the context of an entirely different set of beliefs, one that brings you strength and hope. We respect and honor your experience and in no way want to diminish its importance or meaning in your life.

We choose to open our hearts and minds to the work of what Christians call the Holy Spirit, or what some Eastern cultures refer to as qi (pronounced "chee"), the life force or vital energy. With either metaphor, the challenge is to embrace the wisdom found in Psalm 46:10: "Be still and know that I am God." When we do this, the Holy Spirit, or qi, flows through us without interruption, touching us deeply and energizing us for service to others. It allows us joyfully to embrace and live the great commandments of Jesus: to first love God the Creator above all else, and then to love those who cross our path as we love ourselves.

While Christianity offers many pathways to a deeper understanding of spirituality, these pathways are often hard to find. For example, some churches base their belief system on the exclusion of nonbelievers, which for many people seems an outright contradiction in the journey toward compassion, service, inner peace, and healing. Although tradition and ritual are an important part of the Christian faith, many Christians feel that rituals have lost their meaning. The words *compassion, social justice, healing,* and *inclusiveness* are frequently spoken in Christian liturgy, yet they sometimes seem disconnected from the daily practice of the church and its members. The energy and resources of congregations seem directed primarily to organizational maintenance, comfort, and survival, leaving little room to nurture deeper practices of healing and spirituality, let alone social outreach programs that address fundamental issues of justice and fairness.

Despite the obstacles that are sometimes created by the organized church bureaucracy, it is possible to foster a deeper spiritual experience within the Christian tradition. A specific technique that Mark and I use is called centering prayer. This is an ancient practice that represents a far more contemplative and meditative form of prayer than what is commonly experienced in contemporary churches. The ongoing practice of centering prayer allows us to feel the presence of God and listen to the Creator-given strength and wisdom within us.

> *The more we empty ourselves, the more room we give*
> *   God to fill us.*
> *Riches, material or spiritual, can suffocate you if they*
> *   are not used in the right way.*
> *Remain as "empty" as possible so that God can fill you.*
> *   God is the friend of silence.*
> *   The fruit of silence is faith.*
> *   The fruit of faith is prayer.*
> *   The fruit of prayer is love.*
> *   The fruit of love is service.*
> *   The fruit of service is silence.*
>
> *   – Mother Teresa*

Father Thomas Keating, in his book *Open Mind, Open Heart,* emphasizes that centering prayer is not meant to replace more traditional prayer; rather, it can put other forms of prayer in a new and fuller perspective. Where most traditional prayer is "talking to or at God," centering prayer is silencing your mind to be fully present so you can listen to the wisdom of God within.

Centering prayer consists of four essential steps:

1. *Choose a sacred word as the symbol of your intention* to consent to God's presence and action within. Examples might be: Lord, Jesus, Father, Mother, love, peace, mercy, silence, trust, or shalom.

2. *Sitting comfortably with eyes closed, settle briefly* and silently introduce the sacred word as the symbol of your consent to God's presence and action within.

3. *When you become aware of thoughts, return ever so* gently to the sacred word.

4. *At the end of the prayer period (which can last* from ten to twenty minutes twice a day, or even longer), remain in silence with eyes closed for a couple of minutes.

The following are meditations from Christian scripture:

•

Blessed are they
that hunger and thirst
for righteousness,
for they shall be filled.

•

Blessed are the poor and humble in spirit,
for theirs is the kingdom of heaven.

•

Blessed are the merciful,
for they shall obtain mercy.

•

Blessed are the pure in heart,
for they shall see God.

•

Blessed are the peacemakers,
for they shall be called
the children of God.

•

The kingdom of God is within you.

•

Seek first the kingdom of God,
and his righteousness;
and all these things
shall be added unto you.

•

Do unto others as you
would have them do unto you.

•

It is more blessed to give than receive.

•

First, love God above all else, then,
love your neighbor as yourself.

•

If you have conflict with another,
before offering your gift at the altar,
first go and be reconciled to your brother or sister,
and then come back and offer your gift to God.

•

Putting away lying, speak to all persons with truth,
for we are all connected.

•

As you become upset with another person and
judgmental, first take the log out of your own eye,
and then you will see clearly to take the speck
out of your brother or sister's eye.

•

Overcome evil with good.

•

Whatever you sow, so shall you reap.

•

For what have you profited if you shall
gain the world and lose your own soul?

•

For I know the plans I have for you,
says the Lord,
plans for welfare and not for evil,
to give you a future and a hope.
Then you will call upon me
and come and pray to me,
and I will hear you.
You will seek me and find me;
when you seek me with all your heart.

•

Be kind to one another, tenderhearted,
forgiving one another.

•

You cannot serve God and Mammon (money, greed).
Wherever your treasure is, there is where your heart is.

•

Judge not, and you shall not be judged;
condemn not, and you shall not be condemned;
forgive, and you shall be forgiven.

•

Let not the sun go down upon your anger.

•

I love thee, O Lord, my strength.
The Lord is my rock, and my fortress, and my deliverer,
My God, my rock, in whom I take refuge, my shield,
and the horn of my salvation, my stronghold.
I call upon the Lord, who is worthy to be praised.

•

God is love, and the person who abides in love
abides in God, and God abides in that person.

•

God is our refuge and strength, a very present help in trouble. Therefore we will not fear though the earth should change, though the mountains shake in the heart of the sea; though its waters roar and foam, though the mountains tremble with its turmoil.

•

The Lord is my shepherd, I shall not want.
He makes me lie down in green pastures,
He leads me beside the still waters.
He restores my soul.
He leads me in the paths of
righteousness for His name's sake.
Yea, though I walk through the
valley of the shadow of death,
I will fear no evil, for You are with me;
Your rod and your staff they comfort me.
You prepare a table before me
in the presence of my enemies.
You anoint my head with oil; my cup runs over.
Surely goodness and mercy will follow me all the
days of my life and I will dwell
in the house of the Lord forever.

JEWISH TRADITION

The Christian tradition that Mark and I grew up with is intertwined with the history of Judaism; yet, in our earlier years we had little exposure to the rich wisdom of this ancient faith. Judaism was founded in 2,000 B.C. by Abraham, Isaac, and Jacob and stems from the descendants of Judah in Judea. The Jewish faith is grounded in the belief that there is one God who is the creator of the universe and who leads His people, the Jews, by speaking through prophets. Judaism teaches that the word of God is revealed through the Hebrew Bible (Old Testament), particularly that part known as the Torah. Within Judaism, it is believed that the human condition can be improved, that the letter and spirit of the Torah must be followed, and that a state of paradise will eventually come to the world through the Messiah.

In early Judaism, the mystical tradition of kabbalah emerged. Kabbalah is grounded in the Tree of Life and the Ten Gates of intention, wisdom, understanding, compassion, strength, harmony, success, glory, creativity, and nobility. In the contemporary world, kabbalah is increasingly practiced by those who wish to deepen their own spiritual journey. In fact, after reading *Miraculous Living: A Guided Journey in Kabbalah through the Ten Gates of the Tree of Life,* by Rabbi Shoni Labowitz, we discovered that the wisdom of kabbalah closely mirrors our own spirituality.

The following meditations come out of Jewish tradition:

•

Do not do to others what is hurtful to you.

•

Speak the truth to your neighbor;
execute the judgment of truth and peace in your gates.

•

Blessed are they that consider the poor;
the Lord will deliver them in time of trouble.

•

A soft answer turns away wrath,
but a harsh word stirs up anger.
How beautiful upon the mountains
are the feet of those who bring
good tidings, who publish peace.

•

Acts of love are worth as much as
all the commandments of the law.

•

They who are slow to anger
are better than the mighty,
and they who rule their spirit
are better than they who take a city.

•

How much better it is to get wisdom than gold!
And to get understanding rather than silver.

•

Do not judge your neighbor
until you are in his or her place.

•

They who are slow to anger are wise,
but they who have a quick temper are foolish.

•

For the mountains may depart and the hills be removed;
but God's grace will not depart from you.

•

God is filled with compassion and mercy,
slow to anger and abundant in love and truth,
the One who administers greatness to thousands and
forgives our transgressions.

•

Those who pray for others
will see their own desires fulfilled.

•

The most beautiful thing you can do is forgive a wrong.

•

My God, the soul you placed within me is pure.
You created it, you fashioned it,
you breathed it into me, and you protect it.

•

Above all that you hold dear,
watch over your heart,
for from it comes life.

•

When you insult another you insult yourself,
for you reveal your own defect.

•

Fear not, for I am with you.
Be not dismayed, for I am your God.
I will strengthen you, I will help you.

ISLAMIC TRADITION

With 840 million followers, Islam is among the largest world religions, and perhaps one of the most misunderstood. Christianity and Judaism are closely intertwined with Islam. All three religions are monotheistic, originating from the same ancestors and region. The Muslim faith has a rich and beautiful heritage that offers a wealth of inspirational teachings. We were first introduced to Islam by a close friend from Afghanistan who fled his country many years ago to enter America as a refugee.

Islam was founded by the prophet Mohammed in 610 A.D. upon his receipt of the Koran (holy scriptures of Islam) from Allah. The word *Islam* in Arabic means "submission to God." Muslims believe that Mohammed is the last in a long line of holy prophets that included Adam, Abraham, Moses, and Jesus. Muslims are devoted to the worship of Allah through the Five Pillars: the statement "There is no god but Allah, and Mohammed is his prophet"; prayer, conducted five times a day while facing Mecca; the giving of alms; the keeping of the fast of Ramadan during the ninth month of the Muslim year; and, if possible, conducting a pilgrimage at least once to Mecca.

In the meditations from Islamic tradition, Mark and I hear the teachings of Jesus echoed from a different cultural and spiritual perspective.

The following meditations represent the wisdom of Islam:

•

God does not look at your outward appearance,
but at your heart and your works.

•

Act toward others as you wish to have them act
toward you; and reject for others what
you would reject for yourself.

•

The poor, the orphan, the prisoner—
feed them for the love of God alone.
Don't ask for a reward, or even for thanks.

•

Every breath you take
is another step toward your destiny.

•

Physical health comes from having little envy.

•

Return evil with good, for what act is better
than fasting, charity, and prayer?
Making peace between enemies.

•

If you find pleasure in the good you do
and are saddened by the evil you do,
then you are a true believer.

•

You are not rich when you have material wealth,
but when you have a contented mind.

•

Be patient and you will succeed,
even if it takes a long time.

•

Generosity toward others is your best medicine.

•

There are two kinds of patience:
patience in the face of what you dislike,
and patience in the absence of what you like.

•

Give what you can, even if it is very little,
for it is worse to give nothing at all.

•

It is a failure not to make friends,
but an even bigger failure to lose
the friends you have made.

•

Don't be embarrassed to say you don't know something
or to learn what you don't know.

•

The world is a temporary place.
And the people in it are of two sorts:
those who sell their soul and ruin it,
and those who redeem their soul and free it.

•

Truth is heavy, but wholesome;
falsehood is light but poisonous.

•

Often when we fear that something bad will happen to
us, the fear turns out to be worse than the thing itself.

NATIVE AMERICAN TRADITIONS

Most Americans have a limited and distorted understanding of Native American cultures. Mark and I were introduced to this rich spirituality through the beautiful flute music of Carlos Nakai, of Navajo-Ute heritage. For more than fifteen years, Nakai's gentle and inspirational flute melodies have been a part of our meditation practice, both in our daily lives and in the seminars we present. In recent years, we also have been blessed with a growing number of friends and colleagues from Lakota, Ojibwa, Crow, and Pueblo traditions. They have become our teachers.

Historically, the native people of North America maintained rich and diverse traditions among more than 500 tribes and even more clans, dating back over 8,000 years. When the Europeans arrived in 1492, there were millions of native people living in North America.

There is no single "Native American tradition," although there are many common themes to be found. These themes express a profound respect for the earth and all creation. They honor a higher power, celebrate the sacred in life, and embrace simplicity, humility, and compassion for all creatures. The medicine wheel, an ancient symbol used by most native people of North and South America, offers a glimpse into Native American spirituality. It teaches that the four symbolic races (red, yellow, black, and white) are all part of the same human family, brothers and sisters living on the same Mother Earth. It teaches that the four elements—earth, air, water, and fire—are all part of the physical world, to be respected equally for their gift of life. Finally, it shows that each of us have four aspects to our nature that require development and balance: the physical, the mental, the emotional, and the spiritual.

The meditations that follow reflect the depth of Native American spirituality:

•

Our Father, hear us, and our Grandfather.
I mention also all those that shine—the yellow day, the
good wind, the good timber, and the good earth.
All the animals, listen to me under the ground.
Animals above ground, and water animals, listen to me.
We shall eat your remnants of food.
Let them be good. Let there be long breath and life.
Let the people increase, the girls and boys, the men
and women, the old men and the old women.
The food will give us strength whenever the sun runs.
Listen to us, Father, Grandfather.
We ask for thought, heart, love, happiness.
We are going to eat.

— *Arapaho grace*

•

Earth teach me stillness,
as the grasses are stilled with light.
Earth teach me suffering,
as old stones suffer with memory.
Earth teach me humility,
as blossoms are humble with beginning.
Earth teach me caring,
as the mother who secures her young.
Earth teach me courage,
as the tree which stands all alone.
Earth teach me limitation,
as the ant which crawls on the ground.
Earth teach me freedom,
as the eagle who soars in the sky.
Earth teach me resignation,
as the leaves which die in the fall.
Earth teach me regeneration,
as the seed which rises in the spring.
Earth teach me to forget myself,
as melted snow forgets its life.
Earth teach me to remember kindness,
as dry fields weep with rain.

– Ute prayer

•

Teach your children what we have taught our children—
that the earth is our mother.
Whatever befalls the earth
befalls the sons and daughters of the earth.
If men spit upon the ground, they spit upon themselves.
The earth does not belong to us, we belong to the earth.
All things are connected
like the blood which unites one family.
We did not weave the web of life.
We are merely a strand in it.
Whatever we do to the web, we do to ourselves.

– *Chief Seattle*

•

Earth our mother, breathe forth life, all night sleeping,
now awaking in the east, now see the dawn.
Earth our mother, breathe and waken, leaves are stirring,
all things moving, new day coming, life renewing.
Eagle soaring, see the morning, see the new mysterious
morning, something marvelous and sacred, though it
happens every day, dawn the child of God and
Darkness.

– *Pawnee prayer*

•

It is lovely indeed, it is lovely indeed.
I, I am the spirit within the earth.
The feet of the earth are my feet.
The legs of the earth are my legs.
The strength of the earth is my strength.
The thoughts of the earth are my thoughts.
The voice of the earth is my voice.
The feather of the earth is my feather.
All that belongs to the earth belongs to me.
All that surrounds the earth surrounds me.
I, I am the sacred works of the earth.
It is lovely indeed, it is lovely indeed.

– Song of the Earth Spirit, Navajo origin legend

•

Behold, my brothers, the spring has come, the earth
has received the embraces of the sun and we shall soon
see the results of that love! Every seed is awakened
and so has all animal life. It is through this mysterious
power that we too have our being. And we therefore
yield to our neighbors, even our animal neighbors, the
same right as ourselves, to inhabit this land.

– Sitting Bull

•

Hey! Lean to hear my feeble voice. At the center of
the sacred hoop you have said that I should make the
tree to bloom. With tears running, O Great Spirit, my
Grandfather, with running eyes I must say the tree has
never bloomed. Here I stand, and the tree is withered.
Again, I recall the great vision you gave me. It may
be that some little root of the sacred tree still lives.
Nourish it then that it may leaf and bloom and fill
with singing birds! Hear me, that the people may once
again find the good road and the shielding tree.

– *Black Elk, Lakota*

•

Grandfather, look at our brokenness.
We know that in all creation only the human family
has strayed from the Sacred Way.
We know that we are the ones who are divided
and we are the ones who must come back together
to walk in the Sacred Way.
Grandfather, Sacred One, teach us love, compassion,
and honor that we may heal the earth
and heal each other.

– *Ojibwa prayer*

BUDDHIST TRADITION

Our first encounter with Buddhism was through a dear friend from college whom Mark and I stayed in touch with over the years. Bill had been raised a Christian but became a devout Tibetan Buddhist in his early twenties. He has been a practicing Buddhist for nearly thirty years. It was while visiting Bill that we first participated in a Buddhist dharma session (the rough equivalent of a Christian prayer meeting). While the experience was quite interesting and enriching, we continued to believe that Buddhism was not very practical. This perspective changed dramatically over the years as we learned more of Buddhism and its meditation practices. We now regularly integrate Buddhist meditation into our lives. It is, indeed, one of the most practical and life-enriching experiences that we have gained in recent years.

Peace is all around us—in the world and in nature—
in our bodies
and our spirits. Once we learn to touch this peace,
we will be healed and transformed. It is not a matter
of faith;
it is a matter of practice.
If while we practice, we are not aware that the world
is suffering,
that children are dying of hunger,
that social injustice is going on a little bit everywhere,
we are not practicing mindfulness.
We are just trying to escape.

– Thich Nhat Hanh, Vietnamese Buddhist monk and scholar

With 307 million followers worldwide, Buddhism was founded in southern Nepal in the fifth and sixth centuries B.C. by Siddhartha Gautama, who was known as the Buddha (Enlightened One). The Buddha is said to have achieved enlightenment through meditation and then gathered a community of monks to carry forth his teachings.

For Buddhists, existence is a realm of suffering caused by desire and the belief in the importance of the self. To end this suffering, one must achieve nirvana, the state of enlightenment. Buddhists believe that nirvana can only be reached through meditation and through following the path of righteousness in attitude, thought, and action. Before reaching nirvana, however, one is subject to repeated lifetimes that are good or bad depending on one's actions (karma).

Three principles seem to capture the basic wisdom from the teachings of Buddhism: Cultivate virtue in yourself and others. Do no harm, and be aware of unintended consequences of your actions. Tame your mind so that you can be fully present in the moment, for yourself and others.

You do not have to fully understand the Buddhist perspective on life to benefit from its core practices. As noted earlier, the Dalai Lama encourages people of all religions to integrate Buddhist mindfulness into their own traditions, rather than convert to Buddhism.

The following meditations come out of Buddhist tradition:

•

Your worst enemy cannot hurt you
as much as your own unwise thoughts.
Your best friend cannot help you
as much as your own compassionate thoughts.

•

Words can destroy or heal.
True and kind words can change the world.

•

The heart is like a garden.
It can grow compassion or fear, resentment or love.
What will you plant in your heart?

•

We do not free ourselves by our efforts,
but by seeing what is true.

•

Hatred cannot heal hatred;
love alone heals hatred.
This is the ancient and eternal law.

•

Consider which is better:
forgiveness or resentment.
Then choose.

•

If you are not compassionate toward yourself,
then you are not compassionate.

•

Your body is precious.
It is the vehicle through which
you awaken to what is real.
Treat it with care.

•

Sorrow is healed only when
touched with compassion.

•

Happiness is not achieved
through possession or ownership,
but through a wise and loving heart.
Health is the greatest gift,
contentment the greatest wealth,
faithfulness the best relationship.

•

Do everything as if it is
the last thing you will ever do.

•

Learn to let go. That is the key to happiness.

•

Every life has a measure of sorrow.
Sometimes it is this that awakens us.
To meditate is to listen with a receptive heart.
Everything that has a beginning has an ending.
Make your peace with that and all will be well.

•

Take time every day to sit quietly and listen.

•

In times of difficulty,
take refuge in compassion and truth.

•

No single tradition monopolizes the truth.
We must glean the best values of all traditions
and work together to remove the tensions
between traditions in order to give peace a chance.

– *Thich Nhat Hanh,*
  Vietnamese Buddhist monk and scholar

•

Forgiveness is primarily for your own sake,
so that you no longer carry
the burden of resentment.
But to forgive does not mean
you will allow injustice to happen again.

•

Simplicity brings more happiness than complexity.

•

In life you cannot avoid change,
you cannot avoid loss.
Freedom and happiness lie
in the flexibility and ease with which
you move through change.
In the end these things matter most:
How well did you love? How fully did you live?
How deeply did you learn to let go?

•

You do not possess your home, your children, or even
your body. They are only given to you for a
short while to treat with care and respect.

•

Take into account that great love and great achievements
involve great risk. When you lose, don't lose the lesson.
Remember that not getting what you want is sometimes
a wonderful stroke of luck. Don't let a little dispute
injure a great friendship. When you realize you've
made a mistake, take immediate steps to correct it.
Spend some time alone every day. Open your arms to
change, but don't let go of your values. Remember that
silence is sometimes the best answer. Live a good,
honorable life. A loving atmosphere in your home is
the foundation for your life. In disagreements with
loved ones, deal only with the current situation. Don't
bring up the past. Share your knowledge. It's a way to
achieve immortality. Be gentle with the earth.

*– His Holiness the Dalai Lama,
spiritual leader of Tibetan Buddhism*

HINDU TRADITION

Mother Teresa referred to the Hindu nation of India as a spiritually rich land, despite its material poverty, in contrast to the spiritual poverty of America in the midst of its enormous material wealth. Mark and I have only recently begun to learn more about the spiritual practices within the Hindu faith. Over the years we have known a small number of Hindu friends and students who have led us to want to learn more of this ancient tradition.

With 648 million followers, Hinduism developed in 1,500 B.C. out of the indigenous religions of India as well as the Aryan religions brought to India. Hinduism, a term used to describe a broad range of sects to which most Indians belong, is codified in its sacred scriptures, the Vedas and the Upanishads. The focus of Hinduism is threefold: release from repeated reincarnation through the practice of yoga, adherence to Vedic scriptures, and devotion to a personal guru. Hindus worship a number of deities including the divine trinity, representing the cyclical nature of the universe: Brahma (the creator), Vishnu (the preserver), and Shiva (the destroyer).

The meditations that follow represent Hindu tradition:

•

Knowledge is the best treasure;
learning the record of the revered.
Learning alone enables us
to better the conditions of friends and family.
Knowledge is the holiest of the holies,
the god of the gods,
and commands respect of crowned heads;
shorn of it we are but animals.

•

Treat others as you would want yourself to be treated.
Do nothing to your neighbor that you would not want
your neighbor to do to you.

•

He is the one God hidden in all beings, all-pervading,
the Self within all beings, watching over all worlds,
dwelling in all beings, the witness, the perceiver.

·

Bounteous are they who give to the beggars
who come to them feeble and in want of food.

·

God bides hidden in the hearts of all.

·

Conquer rage with kindness,
malice with goodness,
meanness with generosity,
deceit with the truth.

·

The noble-minded dedicate themselves
to promoting peace and happiness in others—
even in those who have injured them.

•

Study the words, but look to the thought behind them.
Once you have found it, throw the words away
as chaff when you have sifted out the grain.

•

You cannot gather what you do not sow;
as you plant the tree, so it will grow.

•

They who give up anger attain to God.
Do not hurt others,
do no one injury by thought or deed,
utter no word to pain your fellow creatures.

•

Deep within abides a life that will endure
when all created things have passed away.

•

The individual soul is nothing
other than the universal soul.

•

Supreme Lord!
Lord of warmth and light,
of life and consciousness,
that knows all,
guide us by the right path to happiness,
and give us strength and will to war against the sins
that rage in us and lead us astray.
We bow in reverence and prayer to Thee.
Aum.

•

Look on your neighbors as yourself.

TAOIST TRADITION

Recently, we traveled to China with a delegation of Americans in order to learn the ancient healing techniques of qigong, taught by Taoist masters at the Xi Yuan hospital in Beijing. In the daily work with our teachers, we often felt the presence of a deep spiritual power, similar to the presence of Christ that we have felt periodically within our own cultural context.

The Chinese word for "busy" is composed of two characters: "heart" and "killing." When we make ourselves so busy that we are always rushing around trying to get this or that "done" or "over with," we kill something vital in ourselves, and we smother the quiet wisdom of our heart.

When we invest our work with judgment and impatience, always striving for speed and efficiency, we lose the capacity to appreciate the million quiet moments that may bring us peace, beauty, or joy.

As we seek salvation through our frantic productivity and accomplishments, we squander the teachings that may be present in this very moment, in the richness of this particular breath.

In the book of Ecclesiastes, there is a proverb: "Better one hand full of quiet than two hands full of striving after wind." Unpracticed in the art of quiet, we hope to find our safety, our belonging, and our healing by increasing our levels of accomplishment. But our frantic busyness actually makes us deaf to what is healing and sacred, both in ourselves and in one another.

– *Wayne Muller,* Legacy of the Heart

Taoism, which represents both a philosophy and a religion, was founded in China by Lao-tzu, who is said to have been born in 604 B.C. The teachings of Taoism derive primarily from the Tao Te Ching, which claims that the universe is ever-changing and that it follows the Tao, or "the way." It is believed that the Tao can be known only by emulating its effortless simplicity and quietude. Taoism teaches people to live simply, spontaneously, and in close touch with nature. The practice of meditation is central to making contact with the Tao.

Like Buddhism and Hinduism, Taoism is not a monotheistic religion focusing on one god or creator. Temples and monasteries that are maintained by Taoist priests are important to many Taoist sects in China. However, Taoism has been strongly discouraged by the People's Republic of China, though elements of it continue to flourish in China and Taiwan.

The simple words of Lao-tzu contain the same message that Jesus later gave in the Sermon on the Mount, where he spoke of the importance of not worrying about the clothes you wear or the food you eat, for the Lord will provide. Lao-tzu proclaims, "He who knows enough is enough will always have enough."

These meditations capture the wisdom of Taoist tradition:

•

The way to use life is to do nothing through acting,
The way to use life is to do everything through being.

•

Thirty spokes are made one by holes in a hub,
By vacancies joining them for a wheel's use;
The use of clay in molding pitchers
Comes from the hollow of the absence;
Doors, windows, in a house,
Are used for their emptiness:
Thus we are helped by what is not
To use what is.

•

Mastering others requires force;
mastering yourself requires strength.

•

Respond to cruelty with kindness.

•

If you know others, you are perceptive;
If you know yourself, you are wise.

•

If you overcome others, you are strong;
If you overcome yourself, you are mighty.

•

Help others without asking anything in return.
Give to others without regretting
or begrudging your gift.
Then you are good.

•

Those who are attached to things will suffer.
Those who save will lose.
Those who are content will never be disappointed.
Those who know when to stop
will never find themselves in trouble.

•

Without form there is no desire.
Without desire there is tranquility.

•

When you stay behind, you are ahead.
When you are detached, you are at one with all.
When you are selfless, you attain fulfillment.

•

Empty your mind of everything.
Let the mind be at peace.

•

Love the world as you love yourself;
then can you truly care for all things.

Finding Your Pathway to Spirituality

- *If you grew up within a specific religious tradition,* anchor your spiritual journey in the core wisdom of that tradition, even if you have a difficult time with the dogma or current practices of that tradition.

- *If you did not grow up within a specific religious* tradition, find a new path in which you can anchor your spiritual journey.

- *Allow yourself to be enriched by the wisdom of other* spiritual traditions while staying grounded in your own, to the extent that you are able.

- *Be aware of "false prophets" in both traditional and* alternative spiritual practices. When a teacher's ego seems to be ever-present, and he or she preaches that there is only one way—the teacher's way—be cautious. There may be some wisdom in the message, but don't get too attached to the messenger.

- *Anchor your entire journey, your judgment of* yourself and others, in a spirit of humility and compassion.

- *Learn to recognize and trust your intuition.*

- *Own and nurture your spirituality, but avoid pushing* it on others or making assumptions about the spiritual needs of others.

- *Accept the reality that we simply can't always* explain why certain good or bad things happen to others or ourselves. Avoid the arrogance of assuming that if we can't explain or empirically validate it, then the phenomenon simply isn't real.

- *Learn to live more in the present moment through* quieting your mind and slowing down.

- *Don't give conflicts with others more toxic power in* your life by hanging on to your anger or allowing it to escalate. Learn to let go of what is not in your control (i.e., another person's behavior).

- *Remember, one of the greatest spiritual gifts you can* give yourself is the forgiveness of others, especially in deeply painful situations.

- *Avoid going to bed in the evening with anger in your* heart toward those you love.

- *Find a project that provides people with hope and* support. To regularly serve as a volunteer touches your heart, feeds your soul, and helps keep life in perspective. Regular service to others, particularly to those who are different from you and who are suffering intensely, is perhaps the most powerful pathway to deepening your spiritual practice.

- *Learn to speak and listen with the heart, withholding* quick judgment so you can receive the deeper meaning of what is said.

- *Recognize that moments of great suffering can lead* to moments of great healing and growth, even if this learning occurs long after the suffering has ended.

- *Remember that spiritual growth is nurtured when* regular practice (prayer, meditation, yoga, reading of meditations and scriptures) is integrated into daily life.

- *Embrace the practice of living a balanced life that* addresses your physical, emotional, spiritual, and relational needs . . . and includes a good deal of humor and play, as well.

- *Always remember, in its most simple form, the essence* of a spiritual journey is to slow down, quiet the mind, and embrace the sacredness of each moment and of all creation. This requires three important disciplines: practice, practice, and more practice. Eventually, your pathway to a deeper spirituality (whether prayer, meditation, or mindful living) will become a regular internal experience, an integral part of your daily thoughts, feelings, and actions.

You are a child of the universe,
No less than the trees and the stars, and
You have a right to be here.
And whether or not it is clear to you,
No doubt the universe is unfolding as it should.
Therefore, be at peace with God,
Whatever you conceive Him to be,
And whatever your labors and aspirations,
In the noisy confusion of life,
Keep peace with your soul.

— from "Desiderata," by Max Ehrmann

Terms You May Encounter on Your Healing Journey

Acupressure originated in China over 5,000 years ago. It is based on the belief that a person's health depends on having a balanced qi (invisible life energy) that flows through the body. Acupres-sure uses gentle but firm pressure on specific points in the body (called acupoints) to remove energy blockages and restore qi. There are 365 commonly used acupoints. Stimulating the acupoints can relieve pain and nausea, improve circulation, ease tension and stress, enhance immune function, decrease heart rate and blood pressure, and improve sleeping patterns.

Acupuncture is based on the same principles as acupressure. In this technique, needles are placed at the acupoints to remove energy blockages, which may lead to illness.

Aromatherapy is the therapeutic use of essential oils extracted from flowers, leaves, roots, and stems. Aromas may be inhaled, or oils may be either ingested (with proper medical guidance only) or applied to the skin. Aromatherapy is used to treat conditions ranging from infections and skin disorders to immune deficiencies and stress.

Ayurvedic medicine is an ancient medicine system based on Hindu philosophy. It embraces the concept of an energy force in the body (similar to qi) and emphasizes the balance of mind, body, and spirit to maintain health.

Centering prayer is a type of contemplative prayer from Christian tradition. The individual focuses on a sacred word to quiet the mind as a symbol of consent to God's presence and action within.

Craniosacral therapy uses gentle pressure—no more than the weight of a nickel—to massage the bones, membranes, and fluids of the skull and spinal column. These manipulations will reduce tension and counteract physical trauma.

Energy centers (chakras), according to yoga philosophy, are funnel-shaped points of energy extending out from the body.

An *energy field (aura, biomagnetic field, electromagnetic field)* extends out from a person's body. It has some electrical, magnetic, and light energy properties.

Energy healing is an emerging science that uses various forms of energy to diagnose and heal. Energy may be produced by a medical device or projected from the human body to stimulate the repair of one or more tissues.

Energy tracts (meridians) are parallel pathways or conduits for the flow of life energy (prana, qi, life force, life essence) within the body.

In *esoteric healing,* the practitioner places his or her hands above the client's body, balancing perceived weaknesses or congestion within the energy field for the purpose of generating a more flowing, healthy, and harmonious state. *Esoteric* means "hidden" or "further within."

In *external qigong* (pronounced "chee-gung"), a qigong master or doctor projects his or her own qi (vital life energy) to serve or heal another person. This treatment is often combined with qigong exercises done by the patient.

Guided imagery uses the power of the mind to bring about positive responses in the body. It requires the assistance of a trained practitioner. Imagery can help individuals manage stress, prevent illness, or cope with the effects of an illness.

Healing Touch is a blend of energetic healing techniques, including Dolores Krieger's Therapeutic Touch. Practitioners use gentle touch to influence the energetic system, affecting the physical, emotional, mental, or spiritual health of another person.

Homeopathy relies on minute amounts of herbs, minerals, and other natural substances to stimulate a person's immune system and help the body heal itself.

Ki is the Japanese reference to the human energy field.

Life essence (qi, ki, life force, prana, soul, universal force) is the aspect of the person that continues to exist after physical life ends; it is the part of the person that exists before and after life.

Mana is the Hawaiian/Polynesian reference to the human energy field.

Massage is the use of the hands to apply pressure and motion on the skin and underlying muscles for the purpose of relaxation, improved circulation, relief of sore muscles, and other beneficial effects.

Meditation centers around breathing and focusing the mind on the present moment. It allows individuals to experience the limitless nature of the mind when it ceases to be dominated by its usual mental chatter. Meditation is used to balance a person's physical, emotional, and mental states and is an aid in treating stress, pain, heart disease, and other conditions. It is a spiritual practice of several religious groups. Meditation allows the individual to listen to his or her inner self (or higher power) and make the best personal choices.

Mindfulness is meditation in action. It involves being in the present moment without concern about the past or future. Mindfulness is a relaxed state of attentiveness to both the inner world of thoughts and feelings and the outer world of actions and perceptions. It requires a change in attitude: the joy is not in completing an activity, but in doing the activity.

Polarity therapy is a type of energy work in which an individual's energy flow is repatterned through the rebalancing of positive and negative charges. The practitioner places a finger or hand on parts of the client's body of opposite charge for the purpose of balancing energy. Through these contacts, and with the help of pressure and rocking movements, energy can reorganize and reorder itself.

Prana is a reference to the human energy field from Indian Vedic texts.

Qigong (pronounced "chee-gung") is an ancient exercise practiced by millions of people in China and throughout the world. It combines movement, meditation, and breath regulation to balance the flow of vital life energy in the body, improve blood circulation, and enhance immune function.

Reiki, meaning "universal life energy," is a touch technique from Japan. The practitioner places his or her hands in one of twelve positions on or above the recipient's body, then directs healing energy to those sites for the purpose of increasing the individual's supply of life energy.

Tai chi is a low-intensity mind-body exercise widely used in Eastern cultures as an art form, spiritual practice, or relaxation technique. It involves a series of fluid, continuous, graceful, dance-like movements that are performed in a slow, meditative, and controlled manner.

Therapeutic Touch uses the hands on or near the body in a five-step healing process. Therapeutic Touch is one of the foundational techniques used in Healing Touch.

Vibrational medicine is a category of healing techniques that work with the vibrating or oscillating components of atoms, electrons, and molecules, which are the basic part of living systems. Diseases and disorders alter the electromagnetic properties of cells, tissues, and organs, causing them to vibrate at different frequencies. Vibrational medicine works to restore the vibratory frequencies to a healthy state. Techniques include energy therapies (such as reiki or Healing Touch), homeopathy, aromatherapy, and sound and light therapy.

Yoga is a movement therapy that uses posture, breathing exercises, and meditation to reduce stress, lower blood pressure, regulate heart rate, improve flexibility, and create an overall sense of well being.

Books, Audiotapes, Videotapes, and Organizations

Books on Healing the Body

Becton, Randy. *Everyday Strength: A Cancer Patient's Guide to Spiritual Strength.* Grand Rapids, Mich.: Baker Book House, 1994.

This book presents thirty-three short meditations and prayers to offer strength and comfort to cancer patients. The author, a cancer patient himself, understands doubt and depression as well as the debilitating effects of chemotherapy and radiation. He also knows that spiritual and emotional strength is vital for patients coping with cancer.

Benson, MD, Herbert. *Timeless Healing: The Power and Biology of Belief.* New York: Fireside Books, 1996.

Timeless Healing offers a road map for healing and life transformation. Drawing on his twenty-five years as a physician, researcher, and pioneer in the field of the mind/body/spirit connection, Dr. Herbert Benson speaks of how positive beliefs, particularly a belief in a higher power, make an important contribution to physical health. From his perspective, we are not simply nourished by prayer and meditation; we are, in essence, "wired for God." According to Dr. Benson, combining age-old faith, the wisdom of modern medicine, and the aid of a caring physician or healer can allow anyone to use their beliefs and other self-care methods to heal over 60 percent of medical problems. As a professor at Harvard Medical School, Dr. Benson provides an insightful, practical, and inspiring analysis that brings the faith community and the scientific world closer together.

Borysenko, Joan. *Minding the Body, Mending the Mind.* New York: Bantam New Age Books, 1987.

Based on the ground-breaking work of the Mind/Body Clinic at New England Deaconess Hospital, this book shows how readers can take control of their own physical and emotional well-being. The clinic's dramatic success with more than 2,500 patients—having conditions ranging from allergies to cancer—is vivid proof of the effectiveness of this new scientific understanding of mind and body. Using a unique blend of mental and physical exercises, Borysenko teaches how to elicit the mind's powerful relaxation response to boost the immune system, overcome chronic pain, and alleviate the symptoms of a host of stress-related illnesses. Inspiring, reassuring, and practical, this national best-seller guides us to a new understanding of illness and health and shows how each of us can take an active role in healing ourselves.

Carlson, Richard, and Benjamin Shield, eds. *Healers on Healing*. New York: G.P. Putnam and Sons, 1989.

In thirty-seven original essays, some of the world's leaders in healing explore their personal and professional experience in order to uncover the underlying principles on which all healing rests. Rather than focus on diverse healing techniques, the writers seek the "golden thread" that ties together their wide range of approaches. In simple, direct language, the contributors explore the complex nature of healing from many viewpoints. We hear from physicians, psychologists, nurses, metaphysical healers, and shamans. They discuss what healing really is and how it takes place, the power of the healer within, what to look for in a healer, the function of spirituality in healing, the dramatic effects of the healing relationship, the role of attitudes and emotions, love as a healing force, and healing and death.

Dossey, MD, Larry. *Healing Words: The Power of Prayer and the Practice of Medicine*. San Francisco: Harper, 1993.

This book is the provocative, courageous, and powerfully instructive result of Dr. Dossey's quest to rethink his own spiritual life and find what works best for patients. Citing compelling studies and fascinating case histories, he shows how prayer complements, but doesn't replace, good medicine. Specific methods of prayer are examined to show which offer the greatest potential for healing and how temperament and personality affect prayer style. Addressing prayer in the context of many different traditions and faith systems, this book in both insightful and inspiring.

Gordon, MD, James S. *Comprehensive Cancer Care: Integrating Alternative, Complementary, and Conventional Therapies.* Cambridge, Mass.: Perseus Publishing, 2000.

Dr. James Gordon reports on the most accepted and researched complementary and alternative practices, including traditional Chinese medicine, nutritional supplements, herbal treatments, mind/body approaches, and energy medicine. He assesses their efficacy, side effects, and cost effectiveness, and shows how they can best be integrated with conventional care. Dr. Gordon provides clear and easy steps for getting the support you need and creating healing partnerships with your doctors. A special chapter is included on breast and prostate cancer, addressing the use of dietary supplements, melatonin, and soy products.

Gordon, MD, James S. *Manifesto for a New Medicine: Your Guide to Healing Partnerships and the Wise Use of Alternative Therapies.* Reading, Mass.: Addison-Wesley Publishing Company, 1996.

Over the past twenty-five years, Dr. James Gordon has pioneered an approach to healing that synthesizes the best of modern medicine with the best of alternative techniques. This book is a practical guide to understanding the appropriate use of alternative techniques such as yoga, meditation, nutritional therapies, massage, acupuncture, homeopathy, chiropractic care, and herbalism. It is a rich resource at a time when more than one-third of Americans are exploring alternatives to conventional medicine.

Jahnke, Roger. *The Healer Within: The Four Essential Self-Care Methods for Creating Optimal Health.* San Francisco: Harper, 1999.

Drawing upon Chinese medicine's core belief that powerful support for healing, endurance, vitality, and longevity are produced naturally within us, Roger Jahnke presents an easy-to-use program to nurture "the healer within." His methods, which are found in nearly all traditional healing systems, include gentle movement, self-massage, breathing exercises, and meditation. Together, these can help anyone improve health and maintain wellness. The author describes a self-care plan that works without costly drugs, equipment, or experts. He outlines methods that can be practiced ten minutes a day, as well as ten-second "momentary methods" that can be used anywhere at anytime. As a practitioner of acupuncture and traditional Chinese medicine for more than twenty years, Dr. Jahnke presents these ancient methods in clear and understandable terms that make them practical to everyday life.

Kabat-Zinn, Jon. *Full Catastrophe Living: Using the Wisdom of Your Body and Mind to Face Stress, Pain, and Illness.* New York: Dell Publishing, 1990.

This book reports on the Stress Reduction Clinic at the University of Massachusetts Medical Center. It presents a practical guide to mindfulness meditation and healing. Suggestions are directly linked to the goal of integrating spiritual practice into daily life. Joan Borysenko states, "Mindfulness is more than a meditation practice that can have profound medical and psychological benefits; it is also a way of life that reveals the gentle and loving wholeness that lies at the heart of our being, even in times of great pain and suffering."

Lerner, Michael. *Choices in Healing: Integrating the Best of Conventional and Complementary Approaches to Cancer.* Cambridge, Mass.: MIT Press, 1996.

Written by a leading authority on complementary cancer treatment, this book is designed for the patient or health professional who seeks a comprehensive overview in treating and living with cancer. Dr. Lerner is the cofounder of the Commonweal Cancer Help Program in California, which was featured in Bill Moyers' prize-winning PBS series *Healing and the Mind.* John M. Merrill, MD, of the *Journal of the American Medical Association* called this book "a bridge that many skeptics can at least approach. The text is both critical and hopeful toward both conventional and complementary methods of therapy. Physicians will certainly find this book, with its in-depth index and extensive appendices resource guide, the best available single source if they are willing to explore this area." Andrew Weil, MD, author of *Spontaneous Healing,* wrote "If you or a loved one has a diagnosis of cancer, this book can be immensely helpful and can save you a great deal of time and work in determining the best course of action."

Morton, Mary, and Michael Morton. *Five Steps to Selecting the Best Alternative Medicine: A Guide to Complementary and Integrative Health Care.* Novato, Calif.: New World Library, 1996.

This book guides beginning and experienced consumers in finding the most qualified alternative practitioners and the most appropriate alternative treatments. The authors begin by answering common questions and presenting their five easy steps to finding good alternative healthcare. They go on to provide a comprehensive overview of alternative medicine and detail its five licensed systems—naturopathy, osteopathy, chiropractic care, traditional Chinese medicine, and MDs as alternative practitioners. For each system they interview patients and providers, examine insurance coverage, and provide extensive references for further research. Easy to use and understand, this book is a no-nonsense guide to finding the best alternative medicine.

Moyers, Bill. *Healing and the Mind.* New York: Doubleday, 1993.

How do thoughts and feelings influence health? How is healing related to the mind? Bill Moyers travels to both private clinics and public hospitals to examine how advances in mind/body medicine are being applied on a day-to-day level in the hurried and technology-driven world of modern healthcare. He interviews a wide range of mind/body practitioners to determine why their patients heal faster, leave the hospital sooner, and do better once they get home. He also travels to China to explore the implications of that country's fusion of Western practices with traditional Chinese medicine, including acupuncture, massage, and herbal potions. *Healing and the Mind* was produced as a series by PBS television; videotapes can be ordered through your local Public Broadcasting Service (PBS) affiliate.

Rossman, MD, Martin L. *Healing Yourself: A Step-by-Step Program for Better Health through Imagery.* New York: Pocket Books, 1987.

How does your mind affect your health? Based on the latest clinical research, the author explores the mind/body connection to show how to unleash the body's natural healing powers. He provides practical, step-by-step instructions to guided imagery as well as information on how to order audiotapes. Dr. Rossman explains how the imagination can be used to encourage emotional and physical healing; make medical treatment more effective while minimizing adverse reactions; reduce stress and relieve pain; relax completely and recharge the immune system; enhance self-awareness and translate healing insights into actions; and change dangerous habits including smoking, alcohol, and food addictions.

Siegel, MD, Bernie S. *Love, Medicine and Miracles.* New York: Harper Perennial, 1990.

This book presents lessons about self-healing based on a surgeon's experience with exceptional patients. According to the author of this national best-seller, "unconditional love is the most powerful stimulant of the immune system. The truth is: love heals. Miracles happen to exceptional patients every day—patients who have the courage to love, those who have the courage to work with their doctors to participate in and influence their own recovery." According to Ann Landers, "Run, don't walk, to the nearest bookstore and get this amazing book that explains how you can 'think' yourself sick or well. Every family should have a copy. It can be a lifesaver."

Spiegel, MD, David. *Living beyond Limits*. New York: Fawcett Columbine, 1993.

In a landmark study that astonished both the conventional and alternative medical establishments, Stanford University psychiatrist Dr. Spiegel made a remarkable discovery: women with breast cancer who received social and emotional support—in addition to standard medical care—lived longer, richer, and less anxious lives than those without such a supportive community. Drawing on fifteen years of groundbreaking research, the author outlines a scientifically proven program to help all people with chronic illnesses enhance their quality of life. Recognizing the essential connection between body and mind, he teaches these courageous, often heroic, individuals how to face the shattering diagnosis head-on, deal directly with fears of dying, build and sustain networks of support, review and reorder life priorities, strengthen family relationships, improve communication with doctors, and master pain through self-hypnosis.

Books on Healing the Spirit

Albom, Mitch. *Tuesdays with Morrie*. New York: Doubleday, 1997.

Tuesdays with Morrie is based on the true story of Morrie Schwartz, a college professor struggling with ALS, commonly known as Lou Gehrig's disease. Mitch Albom, a former student of Morrie's, provides an honest and inspirational account of Morrie's dying process. This simple, beautifully written little book is full of deep wisdom, humor, and joy. While focusing on

Morrie's journey toward death, the book offers tremendous guidance in living authentically and embracing life with passion. Morrie's last lesson is a true gift to us all, a gift that can lead to greater peace, compassion, and service to others. *Tuesdays with Morrie* is a beautiful tribute to the wisdom that comes with aging and the strength of spirit that comes with openly and honestly dealing with the final stage of life.

Altman, Nathaniel. *Meditations and Blessings: The Little Giant Encyclopedia.* New York: Sterling Publishing Company, 2000.

This small book offers a wide range of meditations and blessings from diverse spiritual traditions, including Bahaism, Buddhism, Christianity, Hinduism, Jainism, Judaism, Islam, Sikhism, and Native American traditions. It includes prayers for protection, peace, healing, thanksgiving, praise, and unity, as well as suggestions for different forms of meditative practice, including mindfulness, centering prayer, energy meditation, and music. An exceptionally rich resource for those on the path of spiritual development.

Armstrong, Karen. *Islam: A Short History.* New York: Modern Library, 2000.

Karen Armstrong, a leading religious scholar, introduces the history and beliefs of the world's fastest-growing faith to a Western audience. Armstrong challenges the idea that the West and Islam are set on a collision course. For those seeking to understand their own spiritual journey within the context of other world religions, this book is an invaluable resource.

Borysenko, Joan. *Fire in the Soul: A New Psychology of Spiritual Optimism.* New York: Warner Books, 1993.

Joan Borysenko, renowned author and mind-body therapist, reveals the power of spiritual optimism, a philosophy that sees life crises as opportunities for personal growth and spiritual transformation. Drawing on her own experience—and that of her patients—she shows how meditation, prayer, and heightened awareness can illuminate the "dark night of the soul." This is the point at which the soul is on fire, fueled by despair. Yet, this same soul burns with an inner flame that can consume negativity, allowing a new soul to be born. The terrain can be dark and most of us need light to find the way. *Fire in the Soul* is that light. The practical wisdom offered in this book will inspire you to shed self-blame, heal childhood wounds, gain strength from adversity, and tap into the love that is everywhere. *Fire in the Soul* goes far deeper into the meaning of spirituality than some people are ready for. It is recommended as advanced reading for those who feel comfortable moving beyond the tight boundaries of orthodox religion.

Borysenko, Joan. *Pocketful of Miracles: Prayers, Meditations, and Affirmations to Nurture Your Spirit Every Day of the Year.* New York: Warner Books, 1994.

In this inspirational little volume, acclaimed healer Joan Borysenko offers a unique path for drawing personal strength and spiritual succor from the wondrous cycles of nature. She shares the ancient wisdom at the core of the world's religions, the guidance of the four great archangels that stand at the gates of the medicine wheel, and her own deep mystical experience.

The book is divided into twelve inspiring monthly sections. Each section reflects such emotionally significant themes as forgiveness, rebirth in love, and spiritual healing. Each section also provides daily meditations, prayers, and affirmations to help the reader release fear and realize the light of peace and compassion that dwells throughout the universe . . . and within the heart.

Cameron, Miriam E. *Karma and Happiness: A Tibetan Odyssey in Ethics, Spirituality, and Healing.* Minneapolis: Fairview Press, 2001.

This book is a highly personal and informative exploration of the connection between ethical behavior, spiritual beliefs, and health and healing. As a nurse and bioethicist, Miriam Cameron identifies the depth of wisdom to be found in both Eastern and Western healing and spirituality. She presents the Buddhist concept of karma and its relationship to both suffering and happiness. A valuable resource for those engaged in their own spiritual journey, *Karma and Happiness* enables readers to honor their own religion while being enriched by the wisdom of other traditions.

Casarjian, Robin. *Forgiveness: A Bold Choice for a Peaceful Heart.* New York: Bantam Books, 1992.

The key to inner peace, as taught by the world's great spiritual traditions, is forgiveness. Many people, however, find this to be an impossible ideal—perhaps even a way of glossing over pain, anger, and wrongdoing. Robin Casarjian confronts the dilemma of forgiveness and offers a new approach to healing our old wounds and self-judgments. As a psychotherapist, she shows how letting go of the past is not only possible, but necessary if we are to achieve lasting health and harmony. This book offers simple but powerful exercises, meditations, and visualizations that acknowledge our hurt even as they lead us beyond it. The author presents moving accounts of forgiveness in action, showing how parents and children, spouses and lovers, workers and bosses—even victims of crime or historic injustice—can all find peace.

Dalai Lama. *The Good Heart: A Buddhist Perspective on the Teachings of Jesus.* Boston: Wisdom Publications, 1996.

The Dalai Lama, one of the world's most beloved spiritual teachers, comments on well-known passages from each of the four Christian Gospels. His Buddhist perspective on the Sermon on the Mount, the Beatitudes, the parable of the mustard seed, the Resurrection, and other selections underscores the parallels between Christian and Buddhist teachings, as well as an extraordinary similarity between the lives of Jesus and the Buddha.

Glassman, Bernie. *Bearing Witness: A Zen Master's Lessons in Making Peace.* New York: Random House, 1999.

Bernie Glassman presents rich and practical spiritual wisdom to help people from all traditions make peace in their hearts and the world. Sharing numerous stories, the author illuminates a number of paths for making peace one moment at a time, even in the most difficult situations. As the founder of the Zen Peacemakers Order, Glassman clearly presents his practice of engaged spirituality and the three key tenets of the Order: letting go of fixed ideas, healing ourselves and others, and bearing witness to whatever is taking place within us or right before our eyes. His work with people from other faith traditions, as well as his application of engaged spirituality through community development initiatives in an urban setting, provide an inspirational model of authentic peacemaking.

Hanh, Thich Nhat. *Living Buddha, Living Christ.* New York: Riverhead Books, 1995.

Billions of lives have been shaped by the teachings and practices of Buddha and Christ. For decades, Thich Nhat Hanh, a Vietnamese Buddhist monk, has been actively involved in a dialogue between these two contemplative traditions, bringing to Christianity an appreciation of its beauty that could be conveyed only by an outsider. In clear, meditative prose, Thich Nhat Hanh explores the crossroads of compassion and holiness at which the two traditions meet, reawakening our understanding of both.

Hanh, Thich Nhat. *The Miracle of Mindfulness: A Manual on Meditation.* Boston: Beacon Press, 1987.

Written for Westerners, this book is a beautiful guide to Eastern meditation and mindfulness—the state of being awake and fully aware. Thich Nhat Hanh's anecdotes and practical exercises show that opportunities for mindfulness are frequent and close at hand: washing the dishes, answering the telephone, drinking tea. His gentle and compassionate spirit and method of meditation will help readers—whatever their religious orientation—achieve greater self-understanding and peacefulness. The author, a Zen master and poet, was chairman of the Vietnamese Buddhist Peace Delegation during the Vietnam War. Dr. Martin Luther King, Jr., nominated him for the Nobel Peace Prize. Joan Borysenko claims "*The Miracle of*

Mindfulness is a jewel of clarity, wisdom, and practicality. Its gift is the transformation of everyday life into an experience of joy, peace, and wonder."

Kabat-Zinn, Jon. *Wherever You Go There You Are: Mindfulness Meditation in Everyday Life.* New York: Hyperion, 1994.

Jon Kabat-Zinn provides one of the most clear and practical introductions to Buddhist mindfulness meditation available. Mindfulness is about learning to live fully in the present moment, to move beyond our tendency to let our busy lives overwhelm us. Mindfulness is at the heart of Buddhist meditation, yet its essence is universal. Kabat-Zinn presents this material in a manner that people of all religious and secular traditions can benefit from. He provides a simple path for cultivating mindfulness in each moment of life. Jon Kabat-Zinn presents both the simplicity and depth of meditation practice.

Keating, Thomas. *Open Mind, Open Heart: The Contemplative Dimension of the Gospel.* Rockport, Mass.: Element Books, 1986.

This book integrates meditation and contemplative practice within the context of the Christian tradition. Father Thomas Keating describes "centering prayer," a conscious letting-go of Small Mind and its continual self-centered fantasies. In this form of prayer, awareness is shifted away from thoughts, which Father Keating compares to boats floating down the river of consciousness, to the river itself. The river is Big Mind, Divine Presence. This is Joan Borysenko's favorite book on meditation.

Kornfield, Jack. *Buddha's Little Instruction Book.* New York: Bantam Books, 1994.

Jack Kornfield, a well-known American Buddhist teacher and psychologist, has distilled the ancient Buddhist teachings and adapted them to contemporary life. He presents simple instructions to finding happiness and peace amid the busyness and distractions of modern life. With its practical suggestions and six meditations, *Buddha's Little Instruction Book* is an invaluable spiritual guide.

Labowitz, Rabbi Shoni. *Miraculous Living: A Guided Journey in Kabbalah through the Ten Gates of the Tree of Life.* New York: Simon and Schuster, 1996.

For thousands of years, the mystical, life-transforming kabbalah has existed within Judaism. This book puts forth its essence in a way that every person, regardless of religious background, can understand. Rabbi Shoni Labowitz guides readers on a spiritual journey through the Ten Heavenly Gates of the Tree of Life: intention, wisdom, understanding, compassion, strength, harmony, success, glory, creativity, and nobility, so that people of all faiths and backgrounds can access the profound wisdom of the kabbalistic path.

Lozoff, Bo. *It's a Meaningful Life: It Just Takes Practice.* New York: Viking Books, 1999.

Life in modern Western culture is often characterized as the "fast lane." Spiritual teacher and activist Bo Lozoff helps the reader discover the "vast lane," which can lead to greater happiness, joy, compassion, and service to others. Lozoff argues that to achieve authentic spirituality, inward spiritual practice is inseparable from the outward practice of unselfish service to others. Until we focus more on compassion for others than on satisfaction for ourselves, the gift of true happiness will elude us.

Lozoff shares helpful and practical suggestions, as well as numerous stories from his experiences in both the East and the West, all of which illustrate the major themes of this readable and insightful book.

McGaa, Eagle Man, Ed. *Mother Earth Spirituality: Native American Paths to Healing Ourselves and Our World.* San Francisco: Harper Collins, 1990.

Ed McGaa, an Oglala Sioux, teaches readers how to reconnect with and heal our wounded earth in this important introduction to Native American philosophy, history, and rites. Specific sections in the book include the spiritual character of the Native American, the seven Mother Earth ceremonies, bringing forth your own Mother Earth wisdom, and healing Mother Earth in your community. According to one reviewer, this book is "fascinating as well as inspiring reading. Ed McGaa makes an excellent spiritual guide and intellectual teacher. . . . The information stimulates the mind, the drawings delight the eye, and the ideas soothe the spirit."

Moses, Jeffrey. *Oneness: Great Principles Shared by All Religions.* New York: Fawcett Columbine, 1989.

The world's major religions ask their followers to seek different paths to enlightenment, yet a universal truth lies along each path. This truth is presented in *Oneness,* a pocket-size book containing the words from each religion's scriptures. The universal principles of The Golden Rule, Judge Not, God is Love, and others act as a guide to inner development, allowing the reader to achieve spiritual richness.

Muller, Wayne. *How, Then, Shall We Live?: Four Simple Questions That Reveal the Beauty and Meaning of Our Lives.* New York: Bantam Books, 1997.

By exploring four simple questions, Wayne Muller shows how we can grow beyond our frequent confusion and numerous limitations to find the wise and ever-present spiritual guide that is alive in all of us. Who am I? What do I love? How shall I live, knowing I will die? What is my gift to the family of the earth? In the quest for inner wholeness, Muller presents true stories of courage and transformation as well as powerful daily practices and teachings from the great wisdom traditions. Few books weave together so clearly the core wisdom of Muller's own tradition of Christianity with Native American spirituality and Buddhism. *How, Then, Shall We Live?* is an inspiring and practical guide to living a life full of meaning, purpose, and grace.

Muller, Wayne. *Sabbath: Restoring the Sacred Rhythm of Rest.* New York: Bantam Books, 1999.

In ancient times, the tradition of Sabbath created an oasis of sacred time, of slowing down in a life of unceasing labor. Wayne Muller speaks of how this consecrated time is available to all of us, regardless of our spiritual tradition. He points out that we do not have to schedule an entire day each week, but instead can have a sabbath afternoon, a sabbath hour, or even a sabbath walk. Sabbath time means getting out of the busy flow of life and work to be more present in the moment and to allow the essential goodness of creation to nourish the soul. Through moving stories, poems, and suggestions for practice, Muller teaches us how the sacred time of rest can be used to refresh our bodies and minds, to restore our creativity, and to reconnect with our inner happiness.

O'Donohue, John. *Anam Cara: A Book of Celtic Wisdom.* New York: HarperCollins, 1998.

In this exquisite book, Irish poet and scholar John O'Donohue shares the spiritual secrets of the ancient Celtic world. Presenting authentic Irish prayers and blessings, he reveals the many treasures that often lie hidden within the soul. O'Donohue traces the cycles of life and nature, drawing from the holy waters of Ireland's spiritual heritage to lead you to a place where your heart can be healed and nourished. It is a place where you can discover your own *anam cara,* your true "soul friend." Deepak Chopra calls this book "a rare synthesis of philosophy, poetry, and spirituality . . . a powerful and life-transforming experience for those who read it."

Peck, MD, M. Scott. *The Road Less Traveled: A New Psychology of Love, Traditional Values and Spiritual Growth.* New York: Simon and Schuster, 1978.

Confronting and solving problems is a painful process that most of us attempt to avoid; however, avoidance results in greater pain and an inability to grow mentally or spiritually. Drawing heavily on his own professional experience, Dr. Peck, a practicing psychiatrist, suggests ways in which confronting and resolving our problems—and suffering through the changes—can enable us to reach a higher level of self-understanding and spiritual growth.

Remen, MD, Rachel Naomi. *Kitchen Table Wisdom: Stories That Heal.* New York: Riverhead Books, 1997.

As author and meditation teacher Jon Kabat-Zinn states, this is "a book of stunning radiance, authenticity, and power. I laughed and cried my way through it, from beginning to end." Dr. Remen shares a collection of true stories of healing, stories that inspire a journey toward strength and wholeness. These stories draw on the notion of "kitchen table wisdom," the age-old tradition of shared experience that shows us life in all its power and mystery, reminding us that the things we cannot measure may be the things that ultimately sustain and enrich us. As a physician, professor, therapist, and long-term survivor of chronic illness, Dr. Remen touches the spiritual issues of suffering, meaningfulness, love, faith, and miracles, all in the language of our own life experiences.

Remen, MD, Rachel Naomi. *My Grandfather's Blessings: Stories of Strength, Refuge, and Belonging.* New York: Riverside Books, 2000.

These wonderful stories remind us that we can all serve and bless life. Through the wisdom shared by her grandfather, an Orthodox rabbi and scholar of the kabbalah, Dr. Rachel Naomi Remen learned to see that blessing one another is what heals the isolation and loneliness in us all. To clarify the difference between helping and serving, Dr. Remen discusses those who use their positions of power and authority to help fix people's problems, then she examines reciprocal relationships based on unconditional love and mutual enrichment. Recognizing that authentic service brings the power to strengthen and celebrate life, Dr. Remen shows us that all of us matter, and so do our blessings.

Roberts, Elizabeth and Elias Amidon, eds. *Earth Prayers from around the World.* San Francisco: Harper Collins, 1991.

This book offers 365 prayers and meditations for honoring the earth from Native American, Buddhist, Christian, Jewish, Hawaiian, and many other traditions. Themes include the ecological self, a sacred place, the passion of the earth, healing the whole, and cycles of life. "Through this extraordinary collection of prayers from all the world and from all historical periods," comments Thomas Berry, author of *The Dream of the Earth,* "we finally awaken to the presence of the divine that comes to us through the Earth and the entire natural world."

Roth, Ron. *The Healing Path of Prayer.* New York: Harmony Books, 1997.

In this book, the internationally known spiritual healer Ron Roth teaches his unique approach to prayer as a form of energy healing. From his perspective, prayer is the key to tapping into the healing energy of the Divine. For many people, however, prayer has become a rather mechanical, rote practice that has lost its basic meaning. *The Healing Path of Prayer* describes in detail the connection between healing, faith, and prayer, including how to find your own pathway to prayer in a way that connects with God's healing energy. Roth provides guidance in setting up a daily practice of prayer that can facilitate the healing of emotional, spiritual, and physical wounds. While grounded in his own Catholic tradition, Roth provides practical spiritual guidance to an ecumenical audience.

Audiotapes

Borysenko, Joan. *Seventy Times Seven: On the Spiritual Art of Forgiveness.* Boulder, Colo.: Sounds True, 1996.

In these two audiocassettes, Joan Borysenko goes back to ancient times when the little-known spiritual principle of forgiveness was taught by Jesus. When asked how many times we must forgive one another, Jesus replied, "Seventy times seven." Borysenko highlights the great significance of forgiveness to our spiritual growth, our emotional wellness, and even our physical health. These audiotapes present step-by-step meditations, numerous historical examples, and related spiritual insights. Borysenko teaches us how to rediscover the enormous power of forgiveness as a cornerstone to our spiritual growth and healing.

Seventy Times Seven can be purchased from Sounds True Catalog, 735 Walnut St., Boulder, CO 80302.

Chopra, Deepak. *The Seven Spiritual Laws of Success.* Novato, Calif.: New World Library, 1994.

As he draws on natural laws that govern all of creation, Deepak Chopra shatters the myth that success is rooted only in hard work, exacting plans, and driving ambition. Chopra condenses the essence of his spiritual teachings into seven simple, yet powerful, principles that can lead to success in all areas of life. These principles offer a practical tool kit to guide the reader toward a more productive and fulfilling personal and professional life.

Chodron, Pema. *Good Medicine: A Traditional Antidote for Suffering.* Boulder, Colo.: Sounds True, 1999.

Pema Chodron, a Tibetan Buddhist nun, shares the gift of *tonglen,* a simple and powerful meditation practice "for ordinary people like ourselves." Through the practice of *tonglen,* difficulties in life that cause great suffering can be used as a way to befriend ourselves, accept elements of our past that we have rejected, and widen our circle of compassion for all. The breathing meditations presented can offer a practical way to cut through many of the obstacles in our lives.

Good Medicine can be purchased from Sounds True Catalog, 735 Walnut St., Boulder, CO 80302.

Kabat-Zinn, Jon. *Mindfulness Meditation in Everyday Life.* New York: Sound Horizons Audio-Video, 1995.

The director of the Stress Reduction Clinic at the University of Massachusetts Medical Center, Jon Kabat-Zinn provides an introduction to his ground-breaking work on stress and meditation, outlining the uses of mindfulness and leading the listener through experiential exercises. Most of us go through life unaware of who we really are, what we're really striving for, what direction life is taking us. Did you know that even five minutes of meditation a day can help you reduce anxiety, achieve inner peace, and enrich the quality of your everyday life? Kabat-Zinn adds a decidedly American flair to the concept of mindfulness—the art of capturing the moment and living fully in the present. He provides down-to-earth and practical methods that will help you wake up to the true potential in your life.

Available in two cassettes at $16.95 from Sound Horizons Audio-Video, Inc., Suite 1527, 250 West 57th Street, New York, NY 10107.

Kornfield, Jack. *A Path with Heart: A Guide through the Perils and Promises of Spiritual Life.* Boulder, Colo.: Sounds True, 1998.

Jack Kornfield, one of the leading meditation teachers in the United States, presents the key principles of Buddhist insight with an eye to the spiritual challenges unique to our time. He offers special meditations, suggestions for integrating modern life into a full and active spiritual practice, and a vision for cultivating the skills we need to see the preciousness in all of life. *A Path with Heart* points to the healing, compassion, and freedom that arise when we open ourselves to the world around us.

A Path with Heart can be purchased from Sounds True Catalog, 735 Walnut St., Boulder, CO 80302.

Muller, Wayne. *Touching the Divine: Teachings, Meditations, and Contemplations to Awaken Your True Nature.* Boulder, Colo.: Sounds True, 1997.

In the tradition of classical spiritual training, this audio course guides you through meditations and reflections to help you find your true nature, cultivate loving-kindness, and live in simplicity and humility. Pastor Wayne Muller says it is inevitable that you will come to a time in your life when you must go deep inside yourself to find the truth of who you are. Often this time of deep searching comes after a personal tragedy that suddenly "breaks you open." This sorrow is also an opportunity to touch something miraculous and whole that is waiting to change your life from within. Muller draws on the wisdom of many of the world's religions to offer a powerful and immensely helpful spiritual experience.

This audio course can be purchased from Sounds True Catalog, 735 Walnut St., Boulder, CO 80302.

Remen, MD, Rachel Naomi. *Final Wisdom: What the Dying Can Teach Us about Living.* Boulder, Colo.: Sounds True, 1998.

In this deeply moving presentation, Dr. Rachel Naomi Remen takes us into the heart of life, where we can learn from those facing death how to live far better than we do. The true stories and insights that Dr. Remen presents will inspire you to celebrate your own life and to recognize your own ability to love more fully and live more meaningfully.

Final Wisdom can be purchased from Sounds True Catalog, 735 Walnut St., Boulder, CO 80302.

Rossman, MD, Martin L. *Healing Yourself: A Step-by-Step Program for Better Health through Imagery.* Mill Valley, Calif.: Insight Publishing, 1987.

These tapes provide an excellent resource for introductory and advanced use of guided imagery to foster relaxation, concentration, and healing. Dr. Rossman has recorded all of the imagery scripts from his book *Healing Yourself.* The tapes can help readers learn to use imagery more easily and effectively. They are available as a six-cassette series, which includes an explanation of how to best use the tapes and a lecture entitled

"The Uses of Imagery in Medical Self-Care," given by Dr. Rossman at a major national symposium on imagery and health. The entire set costs $59.95, although individual tapes are available at $12.50 each. We recommend the entire set; however, if you choose to buy only three tapes, we recommend tapes #102, "Healing Yourself: Using the Tapes/A First Exploration of Imagery"; #103, "Basic Relaxation Skills/Going Deeper Within"; and #104, "Your Healing Imagery/Meeting Your Inner Advisor."

Order by phone with VISA or MasterCard, 1-800-726-2070. Or send check or money order to Academy of Guided Imagery, P.O. Box 2070, Mill Valley, CA 94942. Include $3 postage and handling for the complete series, or $1 for each cassette ordered individually.

Videotapes

Kornfield, Jack. *The Inner Art of Meditation*. Boulder, Colo.: Sounds True, 1996.

Meditation is a doorway to freedom—a doorway that is open to anyone at any time. Step by step, *The Inner Art of Meditation* shows how this ancient practice can help readers feel truly alive and connected with the treasure each morning brings. In this complete beginner's course, Jack Kornfield introduces us to the practice of "insight" meditation. Buddhist monks draw from this same tradition; anyone, regardless of their religious orientation, can use its principles to cultivate a profound inner calm and awaken to the truth. Through easy-to-follow demonstrations, Kornfield presents four complete meditations that you can practice on your own: awareness of the breath, working with body sensations, awareness of thoughts and feelings, and the practice of forgiveness and loving-kindness.

Kornfield is a highly respected teacher, therapist, and author. His videotape can be purchased from Sounds True Catalog, 735 Walnut St., Boulder, CO 80302.

Moyers, Bill. *Healing and the Mind.* New York: Ambrose Video Publishing, 1993.

This series was first aired by the Public Broadcasting Service (PBS) in 1993. It represents an overview of the growing practice of complementary healthcare and its focus on the mind/body connection. Through a series of interviews with nationally recognized practitioners and visits to their programs, Bill Moyers presents an interesting and resource-rich story about the mind's involvement in the healing of the body. The video series, which parallels his book by the same title, can be purchased through your local PBS affiliate.

Organizations

Academy of Guided Imagery
P.O. Box 2070
Mill Valley, CA 94942
(800) 726-2070

American Dietetic Association
216 West Jackson, Suite 800
Chicago, IL 60606
(312) 899-0040

American Holistic Medical Association
4101 Lake Boone Trail, Suite 201
Raleigh, NC 27607
(800) 279-AHNA; (919) 787-4916

American Massage Therapy Association
820 Davis Street, Suite 100
Evanston, IL 60201-4444
(708) 864-0123

Center for Mind-Body Medicine
5225 Connecticut Avenue, NW, Suite 414
Washington, DC 20015
(202) 966-7338; (202) 966-2589 fax

Center for Spirituality and Healing
Mayo Mail Code 505
C592 Mayo Memorial Building
420 Delaware Street SE
Minneapolis, MN 55455
(612) 624-9459; (612) 626-5280 fax
www.csh.umn.edu

Contemplative Outreach, Ltd.
10 Park Place, Suite 2B
P.O. Box 737
Butler, NJ 07405
(973) 838-3384; (973) 492-5795

Healing Touch International, Inc.
12477 West Cedar Drive, Suite 202
Lakewood, CO 80228
(303) 989-7982; (303) 980-8683 fax

Insight Meditation Society
1230 Pleasant Street
Barre, MA 01005
(508) 355-4378

Kripalu Center for Yoga and Health
P.O. Box 793
Lenox, MA 01240
(413) 448-3400

Office of Alternative Medicine
9000 Rockville Pike
Building 31, Room 5B-37
Mailstop 2182
Bethesda, MD 20892
(301) 402-2466; (301) 402-4741 fax

Tai Chi Chuan Study Center
750 Miller Avenue
Great Falls, VA 22066
(703) 759-9141

Washington Center for Meditation Studies
1854 Swann Street, NW
Washington, DC 20009
(202) 234-2866

Yoga Journal
2054 University Avenue, Suite 600
Berkeley, CA 94704
(510) 841-9200

ABOUT THE AUTHORS

Alexa Umbreit is a nurse manager at Fairview Health Services in Minneapolis. She has been involved with the hospice movement, and she has played an active role in introducing complementary and alternative care to a hospital setting. Alexa has a graduate degree from the University of Minnesota School of Nursing, and she is a certified Healing Touch practitioner.

Mark Umbreit is a professor and the founding director of the Center for Restorative Justice and Peacemaking at the School of Social Work, University of Minnesota. He has authored numerous articles and four books, including *Mediating Interpersonal Conflicts: A Pathway to Peace*. Mark has conducted seminars and lectures throughout North America, Europe, Japan, and China. He is a practicing mediator.

Both Alexa and Mark have been trained in Healing Touch, endorsed by the American Holistic Nurses Association, and qigong, which they learned from masters at the China Academy of Traditional Chinese Medicine, Xi Yuan Hospital, in Beijing. They have coauthored two booklets for the Center for Spirituality and Healing at the University of Minnesota's Academic Health Center: *Embracing Life while Facing Cancer: Resources for Self-Healing* and *Pathways to Spirituality and Healing*.